Barbara Hepworth: *a pictorial autobiography*

DATE DUE

			PRINTED IN U.S.A.

Barbara Hepworth

A PICTORIAL AUTOBIOGRAPHY

The Tate Gallery

© 1985 Alan Bowness

ISBN 1 85437 149 5
First published by Moonraker Press 1970 Revised edition 1978
Edited and designed by Anthony Adams
Reprint published by Tate Publishing
Millbank, London SW1P 4RG, 1985, 1993 and 1995
Printed in Great Britain by Butler & Tanner Ltd.,
Frome and London

A note on the 1993 edition

Barbara Hepworth's *Pictorial Autobiography* was conceived by Anthony Adams, publisher
and director at one time of *Studio International*, Cory, Adams and Mackay, and the Moonraker Press. With his wife and children he was a regular summer visitor to St Ives in the sixties,
and became a friend of Barbara Hepworth. He much admired the short texts that the sculptor
had written for the 1952 Lund Humphries book, *Barbara Hepworth, Carvings and Drawings*.
He tried to persuade Barbara to write her autobiography.

Barbara began, but found she had neither time nor inclination to write a long text, and so the
concept of a *pictorial* autobiography was born. She looked out some family photographs, but
this made the book too personal for her taste, so she asked me to help. I added the art historical material, and this helped to give the book a more rounded character - more work than life,
which was what she wanted. Tony's wife designed the lay-out, and it was warmly received on
publication in 1970.

After Hepworth's death and the opening of the Hepworth museum in St Ives I prepared a second edition, adding an eight page section on her final years. The *Pictorial Autobiography* has
remained in print, a guidebook to the Hepworth Museum, and for anyone who wants to know
the essential facts of the sculptor's life. As the Tate Gallery took over the museum in 1980, it
seemed appropriate to place the book in the care of Tate Gallery Publications.

Alan Bowness, July 1993

Acknowledgements to the first edition

For their help in the preparation of this book I wish to thank all my friends; the Trustees of the
Tate Gallery, the British Broadcasting Corporation, Westward Television and Clive Gunnell,
Messrs Lund Humphries, Thames and Hudson and - for their photographs - The Listener,
Studio International, Lefevre Gallery, Ariel Books, British Crown Copyright, Aero Films, John
Vickers, Punch, Radio Times, Houston Rogers, Pictorial Press, Bill Brandt, Michael Ramon,
Jean de Mayer, The Scotsman, Rijksmuseum Kröller-Müller, Holland, United Nations News,
Ronald Sheridon, Serina Wadham, United Nations, Swedish Touring Club, Lars Hansen
Politikan Presse, Penwith Photo Press, John Webb Brompton Studio, Nicholas Toyne, David
Farrell, Fresees Ltd, Gimpel Fils, Arno Hammacher, Peter Kinnear, Keystone Press Agency,
Cornel Lucas, Rosemary Mathews, John Mills, Morgan-Wells, Anthony Panting, Robert
Roskrow, Photo Studios, Lee Sheldrake, P. E. C. Smith, The Times, Whitechapel Art Gallery,
Studio St. Ives, the late Paul Schutzer, Wakefield High School, the County Coucil of the West
Riding of Yorkshire. Some of the author's own material has already appeared in: *Unit One;
Barbara Hepworth* (1961); *J.P. Hodin European Critic* (1965); *Michael Tippett* (1965).

Barbara Hepworth, 1970

Contents

This book is dedicated to Frank Halliday and his wife Nancibel,
who have given me friendship, love and courage for two decades.

Childhood and youth

BORN 1903

SCHOLARSHIP TO WAKEFIELD GIRLS' HIGH SCHOOL

SCHOLARSHIP TO LEEDS SCHOOL OF ART

MAJOR SCHOLARSHIP TO THE ROYAL COLLEGE OF ART

AWARDED WEST RIDING TRAVELLING SCHOLARSHIP 1923

MARRIED IN FLORENCE TO JOHN SKEAPING

RETURNED TO ENGLAND

FIRST ONE-MAN EXHIBITION 1928

PAUL BORN 1929

I was the firstborn. We were poor, as my parents were young, and my father was working his way up from the bottom to the top of his profession. I only remember being loved by my parents, and loved by my paternal grandmother and great grandmother also.

There was a strange mixture of frugality and strong discipline, of early rising and long hours of work and early bed, fused with an unusual sense of liberalism wherein a boy and a girl were equal: and my father promised and fulfilled his idea that his three daughters and one son should have equal educational opportunities.

3 Two months old, with my paternal great-grandmother, paternal grandmother (Allison Hepworth), and my father.

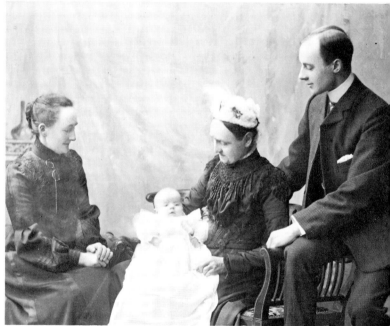

1 My father (Herbert Raikes Hepworth)

2 My mother (Gertrude Allison – née Johnson)

4 Aged six months

My father was, throughout his life, gentle, kind and very intelligent and a fine engineer. He only had to look at me with his expressive eyes to quell my misbehaviour. My mother was beautiful and gay and it was she who saved and scraped to inspire me to further effort in music and dance and book scholarship.

Their lavish love and their necessary stern frugality were the basis of my training.

6 Howarth

7 Aged 2½ years

All my early memories are of forms and shapes and textures. Moving through and over the West Riding landscape with my father in his car, the hills were sculptures; the roads defined the form. Above all, there was the sensation of moving physically over the contours of fulnesses and concavities, through hollows and over peaks — feeling, touching, seeing, through mind and hand and eye. This sensation has never left me. I, the sculptor, am the landscape. I am the form and I am the hollow, the thrust and the contour.

Feelings about ideas and people and the world all about us struggle inside me to find the evocative symbol affirming these early and secure sensations — the feeling of the magic of man in a landscape, whether it be a pastoral image or a miner squatting in the rectangle of his door or the 'Single form' of a millgirl moving against the wind, with her shawl wrapped round her head and body. On the lonely hills a human figure has the vitality and the poignancy of all man's struggles in this universe.

8 Heights south of Keighley
5 (Opposite) Cow and Calf rocks above Ilkley

9

9 I was baptised and confirmed at Wakefield Cathedral

10 County Hall, Wakefield – where
my father worked as Civil Engineer

11 The house at Robin Hood's Bay

12 Aged ten years

13 Wakefield Girls' High School

14 School Certificate, July 1918

15 Aged eighteen at the Royal College of Art in London

THE ROYAL COLLEGE OF ART

SOUTH KENSINGTON, LONDON

THIS Diploma of Associateship of the
Royal College of Art has been awarded to

Jocelyn Barbara Hepworth

who has satisfactorily completed the
prescribed course and has executed a
composition in

Sculpture

Principal

President of the Board of Education

Registrar

day of 19

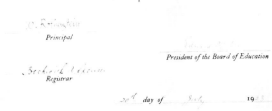

17 Royal College of Art Award of Diploma of Associateship (July)

16 Portrait Head

Wakefield Cathedral, where I was confirmed, played a large part in my early life, and the Wakefield Girls' High School also. I shall never forget the joy of going to school and the gorgeous smell of the paint I was allowed to use, nor the inspiration and help the Headmistress, Miss McCroben, gave me.

She knew every one of her 600 girls and one thing we shared in common was an immense pride in our beautiful school – its fine tradition, the splendid reproductions of works of art in all classrooms, the fine gymnasium, art room, physics room, and above all the sense of each of us being known and loved.

My Headmistress of that time remained my friend for many years. At the age of seven, her lecture and slides of Egyptian sculpture fired me off, and when I approached her at 15 years and said I could not go on with academic training as I wished to be a sculptor, she was the one who said 'You can sit for a scholarship to Leeds next week!'

My Headmistress knew I detested sports and games. I loved dancing, music, drawing and painting. And wonderfully, when all had departed to the playing fields I found myself miraculously alone with easel, paints and paper in the school.

The County Hall was where my father worked (later to become Highways Engineer) and from where I got my Scholarships. And then Leeds and freedom. When I arrived at the Royal College of Art they said I was too young and set me to do a test (16) and I was allowed to stay.

Then student days and trips to Paris. An expanding world.

18 In Paris with Henry Moore and Edna Ginesi
(later Mrs Coxon): photograph taken by Raymond Coxon

19 In Siena

20 Siena (above right)

21 John Skeaping in Siena (below)

22 In Siena (below right)

Getting my travelling scholarship to Italy after my Diploma ARCA was a fulfilment of a dream. I arrived in Florence at night with only £9 in my pocket (and went to an international hostel). The light at dawn was so wonderful in the eyes of a Yorkshirewoman who had spent three years in London smog. This new light seized me and I spent one year just wandering and looking everywhere. I did the unforgivable and produced no work for Yorkshire County Council, but what I saw has sustained me these many years.

I wandered round Florence, Siena, Lucca, Arezzo, basking in the new bright light and the new idea of form in the sun. The whole experience gave me new eyes.

23 Portrait in marble by John Skeaping
(owned later by George Eumorfopoulos,
present owner unknown)

24 With John Skeaping at the British School in Rome

I was married to John Skeaping in the Palazzo Vecchio in Florence, and then lived in the British School, in Rome and where we continued our explorations. After two years John was not well and it was necessary to return home. During this period I really learnt to carve marble, and have loved the quality ever since. I visited Cararra and studied the mechanics of moving weights. John carved the marble head of me — now lost. We travelled home with a few carvings and my favourite birds from my aviary; but we had to leave behind some wonderful blocks of marble.

We found a studio and gave a private exhibition in it. Nobody came until the fourteenth day, and then Richard Bedford of the Victoria and Albert Museum brought the late George Eumorfopoulos who bought about three works from each of us. George Eumorfopoulus remained my friend until his death during the second world war. His appreciation and help enabled us to stage our first show at the Beaux Arts Gallery in 1928.

25 In Siena, 1925

26 *Dove,* massa carrara marble, length 13 in. Destroyed.

27 *Seated figure,* marble. Bought by George Eumorfopoulos

28 *Doves (Group),* Parian marble, length 19 in.
(Collection Manchester City Art Gallery)

29 Cover of cataloque of
Exhibition at Beaux Arts Gallery

30 Drawing, wash and crayon, 1929

Here I must go back in time, as I have not mentioned my nine months in Leeds School of Art. I was hard pressed, as I had to travel in the very early morning and back again at 9.30 p.m. from Leeds to Wakefield and often with homework to do.

It was at Leeds that I first met Henry Moore, his friend Raymond Coxon (both on ex-army grants) and Henry was five years older than I. I felt very young and brash; but Edna Ginesi, later married to Raymond Coxon, was there too and became my friend, and all four of us set off together from Leeds for our three years at the Royal College of Art, got our Diplomas and then travelling scholarships. We were in touch, and whenever we had saved five pounds we went off to Paris to see museums.

28

29

DOVES. *Group in Parian Marble.* By Barbara Hepworth.

The honour of your company is requested at an
EXHIBITION OF SCULPTURE
ENGRAVINGS AND DRAWINGS
BY

BARBARA HEPWORTH
WILLIAM MORGAN
JOHN SKEAPING

from June 8th to June 30th, 1928
10—5.30   Saturdays 10—1

AT THE BEAUX ARTS GALLERY
BRUTON PLACE, BOND STREET, LONDON, W.
Please bring this invitation which admits to the Exhibition.
CATALOGUE (Overleaf)

30

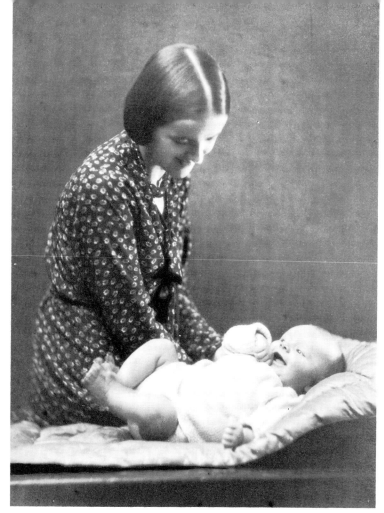

31 With son Paul, 1929

32 Carving of *Infant*, Burmese wood

33 With Paul at Brighton

34 Paul at Hampstead, 1931

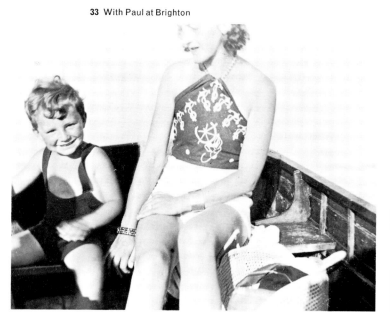

16

35 With my dog

37 Cover of catalogue of joint
exhibition with John Skeaping held
at Arthur Tooth & Sons Gallery

36 *Sycamore Figure*

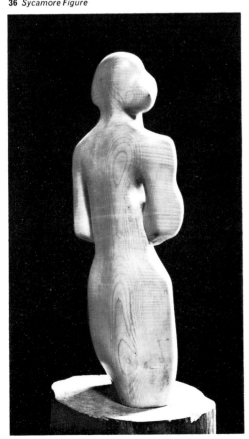

AN EXHIBITION OF

SCULPTURE

BY

JOHN SKEAPING

AND

BARBARA HEPWORTH

October 15th—November 15th, 1930

AT

ARTHUR TOOTH & SONS' GALLERIES
155, NEW BOND STREET, W.1

This was a wonderfully happy time. My son Paul was born, and, with him in his cot, or on a rug at my feet, my carving developed and strengthened.

I did not see what was happening to us after our second show together at Tooths in New Bond Street. Quite suddenly we were out of orbit. I had an obsession for my work and my child and my home. John wanted to go free, and he bought a horse which used to breathe through my kitchen window!

There was no ill-feeling — we fell apart, and finally John remarried and had a country estate and three wonderful sons. John was always kind to me and still is; we keep in touch from time to time.

Friends and relations always said to me that it was impossible to be dedicated to any art and enjoy marriage and children. This is untrue, as I had nearly thirty years of wonderful family life; but I will confess that the dictates of work are as compelling for a woman as for a man. Not competitively, but as complementary, and this is only just being realised.

17

Years with Ben Nicholson

HOLIDAY AT HAPPISBURGH 1931

I MEET BEN NICHOLSON

VISITS TO PARIS

THE TRIPLETS BORN 1934

PUBLICATION OF 'CIRCLE'

THE MOVE TO ST. IVES

I BUY TREWYN STUDIO

25TH BIENNALE AT VENICE

MARRIAGE DISSOLVED 1951

38 The farmhouse at Happisburgh

39 At Happisburgh, 1931 – Photograph taken by Douglas Jenkins showing Ivon **Hitchens,** Mrs Moore, Henry Moore, Barbara Hepworth, Ben Nicholson and Mrs Jenkins.

40 Henry Moore carving outside the farmhouse

This was a period of real maturity. I met Ben Nicholson, and as painter and sculptor each was the other's best critic. We visited Happisburgh and gathered stones to carve, and drew and painted. With us were Henry Moore and his wife Irena, Ivon Hitchins and my great friends Mary and Douglas Jenkins. Henry carved and I carved and my son Paul played on the beach. Work shaped up more and more strongly, and I prepared for my 1932 exhibition with Ben, and Herbert Read wrote my foreword. This was the beginning of a period of what the late Sir Herbert Read called 'a gentle nest of artists' through the 1930's in Hampstead. Sir Herbert was gentle, and I think we all were because we were free and totally and individually dedicated. They were hard times but so happy.

41 Paul at Happisburgh

42 With Ben at Happisburgh

43 At my studio, 7 The Mall Hampstead

These 'working holidays' at Happisburgh were wonderful. We talked and walked, we bathed and played cricket, then we worked and danced. I think this idea of a working holiday was established in my mind very early indeed. My father took us each year to Robin Hood's Bay to stay in a house on the lovely beach. At high tide the waves thumped on the house and spray fell all around us on the balconies. I was always in a state of great excitement. My room was the right hand attic (see page 10, 11) and here I laid out my paints and general paraphernalia and crept out at dawn to collect stones, seaweeds and paint, and draw by myself before somebody organised me! This pattern was repeated in Norfolk, and later in Greece, and several times in the Isles of Scilly.

It made a firm foundation for my working life — and it formed my idea that a woman artist is not deprived by cooking and having children, nor by nursing children with measles (even in triplicate) — one is in fact nourished by this rich life, provided one always does some work each day; even a single half hour, so that the images grow in one's mind.

I detest a day of no work, no music, no poetry.

45 My photograph of Ben at Happisburgh

44 Ben painting at the Hampstead studios

46 Ben reading

20

CARVINGS BY ★ ★ ★

BARBARA HEPWORTH

★ ★ ★ PAINTINGS BY

BEN NICHOLSON

ON EXHIBITION

November 9th—December 3rd, 1932

48 With *Kneeling Figure*

AT
ARTHUR TOOTH & SONS' GALLERIES
155, NEW BOND STREET, W.1

FOREWORD

It is now clearly recognised that the decadence of European sculpture during the last three or four centuries has been due above all to an increasing separation between the artist and his material. A contemporary German painter (Emil Nolde) has so truly remarked that art develops as a continuous chain of little inventions, little discoveries of the artist's own in relation to his tools and his materials. How then could sculpture develop if the sculptor confined himself to tools and materials, to sketches and models, in no way immediately connected with the finished work of art? The revival of the art in our own time is due to nothing so much as to the re-assertion of this vital connection between the artist and his material. To this revival England is making a vigorous and original contribution—a fact already recognised abroad, particularly in Germany; and among English sculptors taking part in this revival, Barbara Hepworth occupies a leading position. In her work the two essential principles of sculpture—the organisation of masses in expressive relation and the revelation of the potentialities of the sculptured material—are clearly expounded without equivocation and without irrelevant compromise. Stone and wood yield their essences to give form a concrete significance. Beyond these essentials, so appealing to our immediate senses, there is a fantasy which should awaken subtler delight in the imagination and memory.

That some of Miss Hepworth's creative conceptions should recede into a symbolic world of abstractions is not a feature that should deter the disinterested spectator: art is a servant (and a redeeming sanction) in any sphere of the human spirit—and not least in this marginal world between consciousness and unconsciousness from which emerge strange images of universal appeal. Probably all the values in art which are more than sensational are in this way symbolic, and modern artists like Barbara Hepworth step boldly in a new venture which may succeed in redeeming art from its present triviality and insignificance. But more simply, more immediately, such art is to be enjoyed: it is perfect in its freedom, its force and its contemporaneity.

HERBERT READ.

50 My carving and Ben's painting

We visited Meudon to see Jean Arp and though, to our disappointment, he was not there his wife, Sophie Tauber-Arp, showed us his studio. It was very quiet in the room so that one was aware of the movement in the forms. All the sculptures appeared to be in plaster, dead white, except for some early reliefs in wood painted white with sharp accents of black, and the next day, as we

51 Article by Paul Nash in *Weekend Review*

52 With Ben in Paris, 1932

Goings On
A Painter and a Sculptor

CARVINGS. By Barbara Hepworth. PAINTINGS. By Ben Nicholson. *Arthur Tooth's Galleries*

USUALLY the association of sculptures with paintings as a gallery exhibition is, from every point-of view, unsuccessful. Even the extremely ingenious attempt to present a combination between the work of Barbara Hepworth and Ben Nicholson at Messrs. Arthur Tooth's Galleries in Bond Street has its disadvantages, but they are of a practical nature only. That is to say, the exhibition, conceived as a whole, has achieved a delightful unity, but to enjoy it fully one must be able to review it alone, and, although that was my privilege previous to the opening of the exhibition, I am both glad and sorry to think it was a unique experience, for this is, in every way, a remarkable exhibition, and everyone who has once seen it will want to see it again.

Before attempting any comment upon individual exhibits, either of carving or of painting, let me try to convey the impression which the association of these so strongly conveys. I would avoid any essay of research into the personal, psychological sympathy between these two artists as too dangerously inquisitive and almost inevitably misleading. There is enough evidence among their work for the eye to form some judgment. We are quickly aware of certain ideals which are shared, certain standards and aims towards which each artist separately directs a determined approach. As a painter, I am naturally accustomed to being asked what I am trying to do, or to being required to say what that is supposed to be. Sometimes these questions can be answered, often not; but the interrogation which demands an explanation of what another artist is trying to do is surely more difficult to meet than any other.

In the case of Ben Nicholson as a painter and Miss Hepworth as a sculptor I would say they are both trying to make things which seem to them beautiful in themselves. At first, this may seem an aim so simple and so usual for an artist that I may safely be accused of discovering the obvious; but if you will consider a number of other contemporary sculptors and painters, in this country particularly, and strictly examine what they are about, you must admit that very few seem to share the pure intention which this work reveals. Indeed, it is unusual to enter an exhibition and be obliged to attend solely to each work, for what it *contains* rather than for what it is in reference to, or how connected with by innumerable wires, cables, railroads, and by-passes over which you have travelled so often before. I was not in the least surprised to overhear Mr. Keene, of Tooth's Gallery, imploring a lady and gentleman, obviously slightly suffering from shock, to abandon at once any idea of looking in the work before them for anything they expected to find. But if the layman may think these pictures and carvings unusual, he may be comforted to know that quite a few professional eyes have blinked before them; and this brings me to a closer explanation of the affinity which exists between the paintings of Ben Nicholson and the carvings of Barbara Hepworth.

I have already referred to their dual interest in making things which in themselves shall sum up a conception of beauty. We should expect, however, that the technique and process of the different media of sculpture and painting would so widely separate the character of beauty as to leave no similarity in the finished achievements. But this is not the case. There remain certain definite characteristics common to both. In the first place, a peculiarity of the exhibition lies in the sense of age which many of

its objects suggest. Miss Hepworth's carved abstractions seem not to have been fashioned by tools, they have much more the appearance of stone worn by the elements through years of time. 'Abstraction' (No. 7) and the lovely profile in green marble are undeniable examples. But when we turn from these to Mr. Nicholson's paintings, we have the same feeling of things weathered and beautifully worn. They have all the charm of old walls or pavements stained and scoured, encrusted with exquisite lichens, enriched by curious and delicate patina.

Another, even stranger, likeness between carvings and pictures occurs in their tactile properties. We are accustomed to enhance our sense of the beauty of sculpture by touch added to sight; it is unusual, however, to judge a painting in the same way, yet, in the painting of Ben Nicholson, there is so much actual texture of surface that we are led to feel with our eyes, even if we can resist the temptation, as I could not, to stroke the hard and polished paint. But beyond these, perhaps superficial, resemblances, these lies a deeper similitude which is the result of a like internal plan. These works, whether carvings or pictures, suggest, as few are able to do, a process of exteriorization. The sculptor has not imposed, but has inhabited the stone and grown within, outwards, as a child grows in the womb. The painter has not applied, but built up from the plane of his canvas outwards, a horizontal edifice of infinitely subtle balance. This is why in both cases we are given a sense of projection which in turn attracts our interest inward to the core of its origin.

In considering these two very interesting artists separately, it would be easy to make certain qualifying criticisms. Both are young, so each still shows, quite patently, the influences through which they are passing or which have been their inspiration. But these are not very interesting matters, and must inevitably be dealt with by those soured chroniclers whose business is to find faults rather than virtues. My own knowledge of sculpture is not sufficient to make me a judge of carving, but it needs little wisdom to appreciate such pieces as 'Two Heads' (No. 5), with its simple, satisfying rhythm and tender forms. 'Woman' (No. 2) evokes recollections of other sculpture, yet is instinct with personality. Each object is purely sculptural—the embodiment of an idea neither literary, naturalistic, nor philosophical, but simply formal: its meaning is itself, itself the only meaning. In the paintings of Ben Nicholson we find the same achievement; they, too, make their own terms with the spectator, who will not find in them a vehicle for sentiments. These paintings, like the sculptures, exist by virtue of themselves; their life depends upon every plane and tone, every line and spot, the very vibration of their surface is their breath. What they presume to represent is negligible; a doubtful collection of mugs and jugs, mythical fish or deformed musical instruments, all equally useless for drink, food, or music. Yet from this curious junk is distilled beauty. You cannot look upon the picture called 'Fiddle' (No. 23) without enjoying it; nor can you stand before 'Abstraction' without surrendering to its enchantment. What known or unknown experience of our nature is touched upon by such paintings needs close analysis to explain, but there is no denying their sensuous appeal. Each is alive with a physical and mental charm, part instinctive, part infinitely calculated. They are the work of a most unusual trinity—an artist, a painter, and a man of taste.

PAUL NASH

travelled on the train to Avignon, I thought about the poetic idea in Arp's sculptures. I had never had any first-hand knowledge of the Dadaist movement, so that seeing his work for the first time freed me of many inhibitions and this helped me to see the figure in landscape with new eyes. I stood in the corridor almost all the way looking out on the superb Rhone valley and thinking of the way Arp had fused landscape with the human form in so extraordinary a manner. Perhaps in freeing himself from material demands his idea transcended all possible limitations. I began to imagine the earth rising and becoming human.. I speculated as to how I was to find my own identification, as a human being and a sculptor, with the landscape around me.

It was my first visit to the South of France, and out of the three days at Avignon the most important time for me was spent at St. Remy. It was Easter; and after a bus ride we walked up the hill and encountered at the top a sea of olive trees receding behind the ancient arch

53 The boat to Dieppe

54 With Ben on the river at Charenton

55 & 56 With Ben at Dieppe

57 Our visit to St. Remy de Provence

on the plateau, and human figures sitting, reclining, walking, and embracing at the foot of the arch, grouped in rhythmic relation to the far distant undulating hills and mountain rocks. There was the sound of dance music — and we discovered a gay café Robinson hidden by trees. I made several drawings.

These were the last I ever made of actual landscape, because since then, as soon as I sit down to draw the land or sea in front of me, I begin to draw ideas and forms for sculptures.

On the way back from Avignon after Easter we saw Picasso in his studio. I shall never forget the afternoon light streaming over roofs and chimneypots through the window, on to a miraculous succession of large canvases which Picasso brought out to show us and from which emanated a blaze of energy in form and colour.

58 Self-photogram, 1932

59 (right) In my studio

60 Alfred Wallis painting

I think the very nature of art is affirmative, and in being so it reflects the laws and the evolution of the universe — both in the power and rhythm of growth and structure as well as the infinitude of ideas which reveal themselves when one is in accord with the cosmos and the personality is then free to develop.

The artist works because he must! But he learns by the disciplines of his imagination. Through moments of ecstasy or great despair, when all thoughts of self are lost, a work seems to evolve which has not only the vivid uniqueness of a new creation, but also the seeming effortlessness and unalterable simplicity of a true idea relating to the universe. In our present time, so governed by fear of destruction, the artist senses more and more the energies and impulses which give life and are the affirmation of life. Perhaps by learning more and letting the microcosm reflect the macrocosm, a new way of life can be found which will allow the human spirit to develop and surmount fear.

61 Ben's painting *Au Chat Botté*

62 Ben's hands

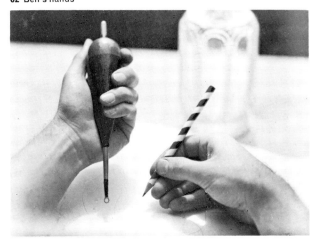

63 My hands

64 Ben's *Painting 1932*

65 My studio, 7 The Mall, Hampstead

66 *Reclining Figure* 1932, white alabaster,
length 12½ in. (coll. Joseph Hirshhorn).

67 Portrait of Ben

68 Article in *The Studio*, December 1932

The importance of light in relation to form will always interest me. In sculpture it seems to be an extension of the stereognostic sensibility, and through it I feel it ought to be possible to induce those evocative responses that seem to be part of primeval life, and which are a vital necessity to a full apprehension of space and volume.

There is an inside and an outside to every form. When they are in special accord, as for instance a nut in its shell or a child in the womb, or in the structure of shells or crystals, or when one senses the architecture of bones in the human figure, then I am most drawn to the effect of light. Every shadow cast by the sun from an ever-varying angle reveals the harmony of the inside and outside. Light gives full play to our tactile perceptions through the experience of our eyes, and the vitality of forms is revealed by the interplay between space and volume.

BARBARA HEPWORTH— *"the Sculptor carves because he must"*

FOLLOWING upon the discussions so much in evidence to-day regarding the arts of painting and sculpture and their place in everyday contemporary life, the Editor has asked two artists of the younger modern British school to state their aims in answer to the questions which are often propounded by the general public.

The artists we have asked thus to present their viewpoint are Mr. Ben Nicholson, well known as a painter of "abstract pictures" in the modern manner, and Miss Barbara Hepworth, the sculptor. The works reproduced are among those shown in their exhibition at Messrs. Tooth's Galleries, New Bond Street, open till December 3.

QUESTION: Do you consider sculpture as an art to be practised separately or in conjunction with architecture?

MISS HEPWORTH: If sculpture was an art to be practised in conjunction with architecture, the sculptor would find other work to do. Architecture does not need sculpture for its construction, nor should the architect be dependent on sculpture for the complete realisation of his idea in building. Sculpture is an additional decoration to the building, and is only lovely when the architect's idea and the sculptor's are in harmony and both architect and sculptor fully realise the abstract meaning of form.

The sculptor carves because he must. He needs the concrete form of stone and wood for the expression of his idea and experience, and when the idea forms the material is found at once.

QUESTION: What is the place of sculpture such as yours in modern life?

MISS HEPWORTH: The place of sculpture in modern life is made by the beholder or purchaser, who is receptive to the idea and life in the sculpture and desires himself and others to experience it.

QUESTION: Why do you prefer direct carving to modelling?

MISS HEPWORTH: I have always preferred direct carving to modelling because I like the resistance of the hard material and feel happier working that way. Carving is more adapted to the expression of the accumulative idea of experience and clay to the visual attitude. An idea for carving must be clearly formed before starting and sustained during the long process of working; also, there are all the beauties of several hundreds of different stones and woods, and the idea must be in harmony with the qualities of each one carved; that harmony comes with the discovery of the most direct way of carving each material according to its nature.

QUESTION: Many arts are developing with what appears to be a public need, e.g., interior decoration, poster design, etc. Is the work of an artist such as yourself apart from this—in a separate category? Is there a relation between modern sculpture and modern painting?

MISS HEPWORTH: If a sculptor is really able to express his idea with all simplicity and a perfect realisation of form in the round, in addition to the freedom of form in space, the balance of one form against another form, and all with an axial rhythm of growth and life, then he is contributing to all arts and giving to all who are willing to receive. Beethoven, Bach, Cézanne and Picasso, negro carvings, all give infinitely because of their life force. The best carvings are necessarily both abstract and representational, and if the sculptor can express his vision in the right medium, the abstract conception of form imbued with that life force, then he is at one with all other artists.

B. H.

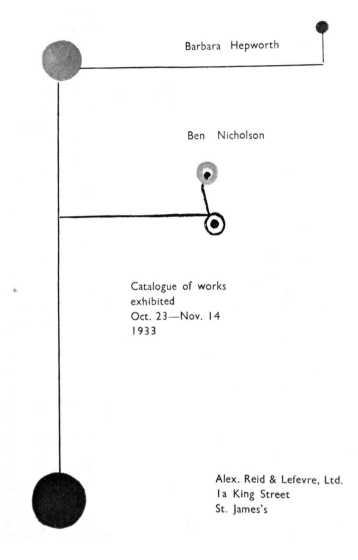

Barbara Hepworth

Ben Nicholson

Catalogue of works
exhibited
Oct. 23—Nov. 14
1933

Alex. Reid & Lefevre, Ltd.
1a King Street
St. James's

69 Catalogue cover of exhibition held at Reid and Lefevre Gallery

70 My photograph of Herbert Read with his son Thomas

71 Article by Adrian Stokes in *The Spectator*

72 Ironstones collected at Happisburgh, 1931-2

73 Cover of *Abstraction Creation*

abstraction
création
art   non
figuratif 1934

3

November 3, 1933.] THE SPECTATOR.

Art

Miss Hepworth's Carving

MISS HEPWORTH is exhibiting her sculpture, carved stone and wood, at the Lefévre galleries in conjunction with Mr. Nicholson's paintings, of which I wrote last week. Since her stone pieces are more numerous, it will be convenient to judge Miss Hepworth's sensibility by her achievements in this material alone. A glance at the carvings shows that their unstressed rounded shapes magnify the equality of radiance so typical of stone: once again we are ready to believe that from stone's suffused or equal or slightly luminous light, all successful sculpture in whatever material has borrowed a vital steadiness, a solid and vital repose. This steadiness of shape, through many ages unconsciously expressed by visual art, in recent times had been altogether lost. To cultivate a reverence for stone thus became an aesthetic need. Miss Hepworth is one of the rare living sculptors who deliberately renew stone's essential shapes.

To the imagination nothing is more solid than stone: we may find reassurance in the gradations of its smooth continuous surface, in its characteristic shapes, if as such the carver has externalized common emotions. The true carver attacks his material so that it may bear a vivifying or plastic fruit. He woos the block. Not Shape, not Form, but stone-shapes are his concern. Stone may be forced to realize almost any plastic idea: but as carving it is valueless if no love, no reverence, has been paid to the stone; however great the merits of the plastic idea, the stone itself has not come to life.

What are the essential shapes of stone? Pebbles are such shapes since in accordance with their structures they have responded to the carving of the elements. They are nearly always beautiful when smooth, when they show an equal light, when that light and the texture it illumines convey the sense of all the vagaries of centuries as one smooth object. Thus a slate pebble, suitable for "ducks and drakes," with an equally lit and homogeneous emaciation, thin yet no wise sharp, suggests an incontrovertible roundness: for it has been worked upon and flattened; a deeper roundness has emerged. Similarly the human carver thins the stone, reveals smooth and gradual forms. As pebbles by natural forces, so forms by the true carver are rubbed: though it is sufficient for him to rub the stone in the final process only.

You may see the rubbed forms from every angle of Miss Hepworth's carving. Any one who gains reassurance from the certainty of smoothed, caressed stone has a great pleasure in store at the Lefévre galleries. These stones are inhabited with feeling, even if, in common with the majority of "advanced" carvers, Miss Hepworth has felt not only the block, but also its potential fruit, to be always feminine. These sculptors approach the block with such gravity that more ebullient, more masculine, forms evade them. None the less, after Miss Hepworth's exhibition, her contemporaries and Miss Hepworth herself, I feel, will modify their attitude. *Composition* (1) caps what has been a trifle too stolid a feeling in our modern carving. Nothing, it would appear, should be attempted for a time on the mountain and mother-and-child themes in view of what Miss Hepworth has here accomplished. The stone is beautifully rubbed: it is continuous as an enlarging snowball on the run; yet part of the matrix is detached as a subtly flattened pebble. This is the child which the mother owns with all her weight, a child that is of the block yet separate, beyond her womb yet of her being. So poignant are these shapes of stone, that in spite of the degree in which a more representational aim and treatment have been avoided, no one could mistake the underlying subject of the group. In this case at least the abstractions employed enforce a vast certainty. It is not a matter of a mother and child group represented in stone. Miss Hepworth's stone *is* a mother, her huge pebble its child. A man would have made the group more pointed: no man could have treated this composition with such a pure complacence. The idea itself is a spectacular one, but it gains from Miss Hepworth's hands a surer poignancy. Her carving is astonishingly mature: whereas the appreciation and critique of sculpture remain fatuous.

ADRIAN STOKES.

A Broado

THE present moment is the only real time. Tradition is no longer a day-dream and things that have been made seem like the unfolding and development of one idea, the growth of some great tree. There is freedom to work out ideas and today seems alive with a sense of imminent new discovery.

In an electric train moving south I see a blue aeroplane between a ploughed field and a green field, pylons in lovely juxtaposition with springy turf and trees of every stature. It is the relationship of these things that makes such loveliness—

The sounds of unseen birds and droning aeroplanes in the sky, part hidden by the leaves of a tree so very much older than I am, the feeling of easy walking down the street with green red traffic lights, the earth revealing its shape to the feet and eye as I once walked up a long white road between trees and saw a stone arch two thousand years old standing on green flat space of earth against stony mountains, olives quietly growing in obeisance at their feet and Café Robinson hidden by trees, the wireless filling the air with music from some foreign station; we can dance at the feet of these lovely undulating stony hills—

It is the relationship and the mystery that makes such loveliness and I want to project my feeling about it into sculpture—not words, not paint nor sound; because it cannot be a complete thought unless it could have been done in no other way, in no other material or any different size.

It must be stone shape and no other shape.

Carving is interrelated masses conveying an emotion; a perfect relationship between the mind and the colour, light and weight which is the stone, made by the hand which feels. It must be so essentially sculpture that it can exist in no other way, something completely the right size but which has growth, something still and yet having movement, so very quiet and yet with a real vitality. A thing so sculpturally good that the smallest section radiates the intensity of the whole and the spatial displacement is as lovely as the freed and living stone shape.

I do not want to make a stone horse that is trying to and cannot smell the air. How lovely is the horse's sensitive nose, the dog's moving ears and deep eyes; but to me these are not stone forms and the love of them and the emotion can only be expressed in more abstract terms. I do not want to make a machine that cannot fulfil its essential purpose; but to make exactly the right relation of masses, a living thing in stone, to express my awareness and thought of these things.

At the present moment we are building up a new mythology which is more easily understood when the things we care for are seen. Small things found and kept for their lovely shape, their weight, their texture and intense pure colour. Objects that we place near to each other, in their different aspects and relationships create new experience. A scarlet circle on the wall, a slender white bottle on a shelf near it, a bright blue box and lovely-shaped fishing floats that rest in the hand like a bird, weighty pebbles, dull grey, some gleaming white, all these move about the room and as they are placed, make the room gay or serious or bright as a frosty morning and nearly always give a tremendous feeling of work—because they are so much a part of the different seasons and varied light and quality of each day.

The predisposition to carve is not enough, there must be a positive living and moving towards an ideal. The understanding of form and colour in the abstract is an essential of carving or painting; but it is not simply the desire to avoid naturalism in the carving that leads to an abstract work. I feel that the conception itself, the quality of thought that is embodied, must be abstract—an impersonal vision individualised in the particular medium.

In the contemplation of Nature we are perpetually renewed, our sense of mystery and our imagination is kept alive, and rightly understood, it gives us the power to project into a plastic medium some universal or abstract vision of beauty.

74 My article in *Unit One*

75 *Large and small forms* 1934, white alabaster (coll. Margaret Gardiner)

76 With Simon

On October 3rd Ben and I went to the cinema in Belsize Park, and my life-long friend Margaret Gardiner had supper with us. Ben had complained a little bit that I seemed withdrawn and concentrated over my pregnancy. But suddenly I said 'Oh dear', and in next to no time I saw three small children at the foot of my bed – looking pretty determined and fairly belligerent. This was an event even my doctor did not suspect, and we had only a basement flat, no washing in the garden, and a kitchen-bathroom, and £20 in the bank and only one cot.

Ben was superb. The day before he had done a three-form white relief. At dawn he did another relief. He was a tower of strength, and rang round our immediate friends at dawn, who said 'Shut up Ben, this is no time for jokes.'

I, myself, knew fear for the first time in my life, as I was very weak, and wondered how on earth we were to support this family on white reliefs and the carving I was doing.

Ben was entirely right and, supported by his faith, our work strengthened in the right direction, and miraculously we made our way, due to the wonderful help given to us by our friends and patrons.

The children were an inspiration, each one giving us a very great joy.

77 Rachel

78 With Sarah

ZWEMMER GALLERY
26, LITCHFIELD STREET, W.C.2

OCTOBER 2nd to 22nd, 1935

1. FRANCIS BUTTERFIELD
2. WINIFRED DACRE
3. BARBARA HEPWORTH
4. IVON HITCHENS
5. ARTHUR JACKSON
6. DAVID JONES
7. HENRY MOORE
8. W. STAITE MURRAY
9. BEN NICHOLSON
10. JOHN PIPER

79 Section of '7 & 5' Exhibition catalogue, October 1935

WHY ABSTRACT?

BY S JOHN WOODS

To the casual observer artists seem to have thrown over the canons of the past and to have divided themselves into opposing creeds and 'isms,' all equally fantastic. There is a grain of truth in such a contention but there is also the chaff of prejudice. In this article the writer asks "Why abstract?" and, in answering, endeavours to show that abstract or non-representational art is not only a logical and inevitable step in cultural evolution but is the art most suited to modern architecture and modern rooms.

Carving in Blue Ancaster Stone
by Barbara Hepworth, 1935

80 Article by S. John Woods; 'Why Abstract?'

New Works by Barbara Hepworth

As a professional archaeologist, the writer feels we must expect ourselves to examine the work of Barbara Hepworth in their native setting. For the fine medium values which belong to the essence of sculpture and which, in fact, characterise good work of all sizes.

Two qualities appear, upon reflection, to be common to most of the varied abstracts of all these carvings. The spatial disposition emphasizes always a three-dimensional effect, and the physical peculiarities of the materials are turned to account with subtle cunning. Both qualities also establish how this desire to contemporary representation of the fine traditions of plastic art.

The method of spatial disposition which Barbara Hepworth has selected may thus be understood by complexity a formal characteristic common to all the carvings reproduced here. They each consist of a monogram that upon which can be two distinct elements are presented. One bounces to call the idea a base, but it be no means so accurately set, on the contrary, an essential part of each element; and it appears but little constructive to a likeness or function.

It appears, then, that each carving contains besides the base and the component moulded elements upon it a third component of equal importance. Even as in many of our the reliefs but also the abstract over nor the surface of the composition in spaces and empty spaces form in their harmony these carvings. But upon examined cannot enter into the order which is a work of art. It is the function of the subtle of this to give a delineate, to define with precision the spatial individuality of each work as a whole.

It is a remarkable achievement that Barbara Hepworth has to say so very near carried to be out of the three elements upon the base. It means that the bar is completely realised all possible interrelations between the elements of these particular carvings that each new grouping, each displacement of the motive elements within the limits of the work as directed by the slab, evinces its fresh harmonies. One is tempted to consider these works as being expressions in which harmonious forms which is pre-eminently death, distinct organic unit with a clarity of

so vivid, even simultaneously, across a large and where in more than the most subtle of constituents.

Perhaps we have carried beyond the veritable material and the non-plastic. If such being qualities of the abstract are at any rate then we become of the similar association to them to do, yet meaning meant and render, in their harmonies and contrasts, the vitalety between their aspects are concerned. What feels it should be stated perfectly that the fundamental, through perhaps but not just a harmony that of scales to establish their dimensions. The one row less great of each quality for a quietly formed appeal which enforces all the very essence that the impetus forced by the object from different, ample charmer, accept the world as empty and upon an ever events it events. Not only the photography suggests the string perfection of a contact when the effective light of the is carried in the hidden adjustment of the work.

It is worth and beauty consider the no matter which enable Barbara Hepworth to achieve a modelling at the surface quite so subtle a quality, as a result of these, worked and contrasted than to make, not only the classic concentration that cut, the effect which its realised contains a force and texture so at is plain abstracts, which proves sufficient, was inspired to express her artful view, to thus merely controlled in the new original objects to the artist arrangement.

By thus actuality in the last degree the force which by decrease in her methods, Barbara Hepworth places herself not less in that context: sculptural traditions that by the spatial sense of her composition and the curved wins of carving which leaves more control to surface textural and harmonic. Abstract carving and these mutual Egyptian works which best can inspire to be invested with a rare of potential moves from a subtle tactile treatment. In her by careful disposition the details of vitality and by one edited work how into her. She experienced the impact of the surprise which the mould curves includes in sculpturing in the entire space between that shift smallest and not being. The sensitive at art in her sense and best but

Illustrations: BARBARA HEPWORTH : Opposite, Carving in White Marble 1935
Two following pages : left : Carving in Grey Alabaster 1935
right : Carving in Serpentine, 1935

81 Article by H. Frankfort in 'Axis No.1':
'New works by Barbara Hepworth' illus. Carving 1935

82 Naum Gabo

846   THE LISTENER   4 NOVEMBER 1936

Art

Constructive Art

By NAUM GABO

One of the founders of the Constructivist Movement explains in the following article the principles of his work

THE word 'Constructivism', as most of the other 'isms', was invented not by the artists themselves, but was given to their work by critics and theorists. The constructivist has accepted this word and franchised it, because it refers to the constructive idea, which forms the basis of his belief. Constructive ideas in general are not rare in the history of ideas; they accompany every creative urge of human development. They always appear on the borderline of two consecutive epochs at the moment when the human spirit, having destroyed the old, demands the creation and assertion of the new. All great epochs have always depended on one leading constructive idea. It has always given the art of the time a social power and ability to rule and direct the spirit of its age.

The art of our own generation was born on such a borderline; it was born on the ruins of all previous artistic traditions. The revolution in art which took place at the beginning of this century proved that it is impossible to impose on a new epoch the artistic forms and æsthetic ideas of the old, and that it is impossible to build up a new creative art upon the caprice or temporary moods of the individual artist. In order to do this it is necessary to have new, stable principles and new constructive elements; these principles must be closely bound up with the social and psychological spirit of our epoch and they ought to be sought for not externally, but in the realm of plastic art itself. We have not had far to go to find these elements. In an article in THE LISTENER of July 29 on 'Reason and Imagination in Art', Mr. Roger Hinks observed that 'the whole European tradition in the plastic arts consists in the affirmation of the Greek Humanist ideal, either explicitly (as by the Romans and in the Renaissance) or implicitly (as in the Middle Ages)'. It does not seem to me, however, that this is the only possible characteristic trend of European plastic art. I do not think that European art can be considered as a whole; there is more difference between the art of the Middle Ages and the art of Rome and the Renaissance than the difference between statement and implication of the same tradition. The art of all great epochs, old and new, has its own defined traditions, and yet they still hold for us such elements as continue to affect us even when their content has lost its meaning and importance. Where lies the cause of this power? It cannot be in the human features of the Greek God in whom we do not believe, or in the image of the Scythian lion, the myth of which has lost its significance, or in the lovely form of the Madonna, or in the torso of Venus.

The value of such images is relative, unsteady and disputable. It is the lines themselves with their rhythms, it is the colours with their tones of light and shade, it is the sizes and shapes with their order in space, their scale and their relations to each other, it is these elements which keep these creations effective and still alive for us and which form the substance of art through the ages. Having realised this fundamental truth all the constructivist has to do is to deliver these vital and independent elements from all their outlived and temporary images and by freeing them to convey the spirit and impulses of our own time.

In the painting of the cubists such as Picasso and Braque we see already manifestations of such an attempt, but this attempt has been made gropingly in the dark: on the one hand their desire to destroy the old prevailed over their desire to create the new, and on the other hand in attempting to create the new they could not free themselves from the external forms of Nature. The constructivist has renounced the representation of natural forms as he is convinced that the external aspect of Nature does not enable us sufficiently to penetrate its hidden depths; this external aspect of Nature represents only the superficial part, the skin of its immense body; it only conforms to the obvious and petty side of our impulses and is not qualified to manifest the most essential and vital subsistence. To be able to illuminate this hidden entity through the medium of plastic art our generation needs other aspects, other imaginative elements and other plastic means. It is obvious that the vocation of the art of our epoch is not to reproduce Nature but to create and enrich it, to direct, harmonise and stimulate the spirit to the creative attainments of our time. Other creative spheres of the human spirit already have this character. Music, for instance, was always free from the obligation or even temptation to reproduce Nature. Nature does not know musical notes just as it does not know multiplication tables and geometry. All these are methods artificially constructed by man for the manifestation of his knowledge and his creative will. As a quality of the plastic element of our constructive art we have chosen the elementary, accurate and primary shapes long ago handed over to us by psychological experience as symbols of a perfected plastic expression. These elementary shapes are universal and available to our general human psychology. In general, there cannot be different opinions as to the psychological effect on a man of a circle or a square or a straight line or a hyperbolic curve, just as there cannot be different opinions as to the psychological effect of the tonic sol-fa in music. Their purely psychological reactions are constant and stable. In spite

Carving in Wood, by Barbara Hepworth, 1935. 'The elementary shapes of this carving and of the Hermes of Praxiteles are the same. In spite of the simplicity of this form, its inner plastic values belong to the same category as those which vitalised all plastics throughout the ages'

83 Article by Gabo in *The Listener*, November 1936

SCULPTURE

Contemporary constructive work does not lose by not having particular human interest, drama, fear or religious emotion. It moves us profoundly because it represents the whole of the artist's experience and vision, his whole sensibility to enduring ideas, his whole desire for a realization of these ideas in life and a complete rejection of the transitory and local forces of destruction. It is an absolute belief in man, in landscape and in the universal relationship of constructive ideas. The abstract forms of his work are now unconscious and intuitive—his individual manner of expression. His conscious life is bent on discovering a solution to human difficulties by solving his own thought permanently, and in relation to his medium. If we had lived at a time when animals, fire worship, myth or religion were the deepest emotional aspects of life, sculpture would have taken the form, unconsciously, of a recognizable god; and the formal abstract relationships in the representation would have been the conscious way of vitalizing these ideas; but now, these formal relationships have become our thought, our faith, waking or sleeping—they can be the solution to life and to living. This is no escapism, no ivory tower, no isolated pleasure in proportion and space—it is an unconscious manner of expressing our belief in a possible life. The language of colour and form is universal and not one for a special class—though this may have been in the past—it is a thought which gives the same life, the same expansion, the same universal freedom to everyone.

The artist rebels against the world as he finds it because his sensibility reveals to him the vision of a world that could be possible—a world idealistic, but practical—idealistic, inclusive of all vitality and serenity, harmony and dynamic movement—a concept of a freedom of ideas which is all-inclusive except to that which causes death to ideas. In his rebellion he can take either of two courses—he can give way to despair and wildly try to overthrow all those things which seem to stand between the world as it appears to be and the world as it could be—or he can passionately affirm and re-affirm and demonstrate in his plastic medium his faith that this world of ideas does exist. He can demonstrate constructively, believing that the plastic embodiment of a free idea—a universal truth of spiritual power—can do more, say more and be more vividly potent, because it puts no pressure on anything.

A constructive work is an embodiment of freedom itself and is unconsciously perceived even by those who are consciously against it. The desire to live is the strongest universal emotion, it springs from the depths of our unconscious sensibility—and the desire to give life is our most potent, constructive, conscious expression of this intuition.

84 My article in *Circle*, published 1937

ABSTRACT & CONCRETE

An Exhibition of Abstract Painting & Sculpture, 1934 & 1935

Arranged by Nicolette Gray in co-operation with AXIS

February 15th—22nd 1936
at 41, St. Giles, Oxford

85 Catalogue cover of 'Abstract and Concrete' Exhibition

86 *Monumental stele* 1936, blue Ancaster stone, ht 72 in.

87 *Holed Polyhedron*, grey alabaster, 12 in.

88 'Abstract and Concrete' Exhibition at the Lefevre Gallery with works by Ben, Mondrian and myself

89 *Sphere and Hollow*, marble, 15 x 12 in.

90 *Form* 1936, white marble
(coll. Charles & Peter Gimpel).

It seemed as though it might be impossible to provide for such a family by the sale of abstract paintings and white reliefs, which Ben Nicholson was then doing, and by my sculptures; but the experience of the children seemed to intensify our sense of direction and purpose, and gave us both an even greater unity of idea and aim.

When I started carving again in November 1934, my work seemed to have changed direction, although the only fresh influence had been the arrival of the children. The work was more formal, and all traces of naturalism had disappeared, and for some years I was absorbed in the relationships in space, in size and texture and weight, as well as in the tensions between the forms. This formality initiated the exploration with which I have been preoccupied continuously since then, and in which I hope to discover some absolute essence in sculptural terms, giving the quality of human relationships.

91 My sculpture, a Ben painting and a Calder mobile

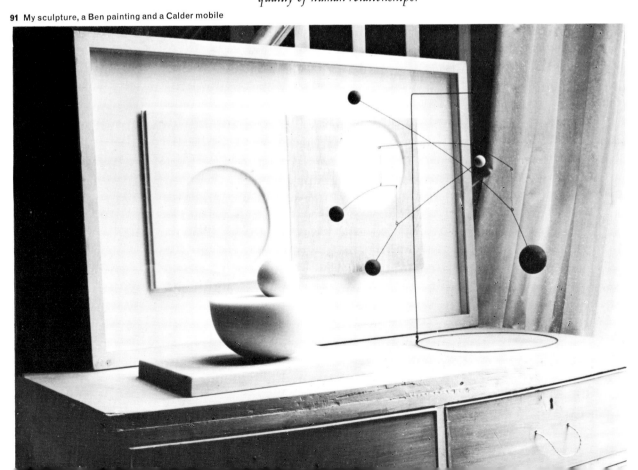

CATALOGUE of SCULPTURE

by **BARBARA HEPWORTH**

OCTOBER 1937

ALEX. REID & LEFEVRE, LTD.
1a KING STREET, ST. JAMES'S

FOREWORD   **J. D. BERNAL**, F.R.S.

This appreciation of the sculptures exhibited by Miss Hepworth is not to be taken as an aesthetic criticism. It simply expresses the relation of an extremely refined and pure art form to the sciences with which it has special affinities. The first impressions of the present exhibition suggest very strongly the art of the Neolithic builders of stone monuments which, in the second Millenium, stretched along the coasts from Sweden to Assam. Nor is the analogy entirely superficial. Neolithic art with its extreme formalism does not represent a primitive stage in the evolution of art, but an apparent step backwards away from the admirable and living representations of the art of the Cave painters. This backward step is illusory, for Neolithic art is highly sophisticated and expresses the realisation that important ideas can be conveyed by extremely limited symbolic forms ; that it is unnecessary to fill in details as long as general intentions are realised. In a sense Miss Hepworth's art stands in this extreme relation to the representational art of the nineteenth century from which the whole of present century art has been in revolt. She has reduced her sculptures to the barest elements, but these elements correspond curiously enough so closely with those of Neolithic art that it is in comparison with them that we can best describe them.

The largest group of sculptures are the upright blocks corresponding to the Neolithic Menhirs which stand through Cornwall and Brittany as memorials to long forgotten dead. Another group represents stones pierced in one way or another with conical holes. Such stones occur in the Dolmens themselves, supposedly to furnish a means of egress for the soul. The most famous of them in Cornwall, Men-an-tol, may be chosen to give them a name. Further resemblances occur in the cup markings and the loose stones which sometimes fill them whose ritual purpose is still unknown, both of which are here amply represented. Finally, the problem of the relation of two uprights or two spheres, many solutions to which are offered in Miss Hepworth's art, correspond on a limited scale to the great alignments and rings of stones which mark the central shrines of the Megalithic world. It would be wrong however to say that Miss Hepworth is simply re-creating a lost phase of art, such certainly has never been her conscious intention. Indeed in other ways her statues correspond to the earliest stage of Greek sculpture recalling many Helladic figures and particularly early statues of

92 Cover of catalogue of exhibition at Reid & Lefevre Gallery, October, 1937 and
(**93**) Foreword to catalogue by J. D. Bernal, page 1 and (**94**) Foreword, pages 2 and 3.

Apollo. In all these there appears a striving for reduction of the elements of sculpture which has hardly elsewhere been pushed so far. In her work we find the concrete expression of the ultimate forms which exist in more elaborate and representational sculpture and may, for all we know, give it much of its value. Certainly it is difficult to say whether we appreciate Miss Hepworth's statuary on account of the prevision it gives us of the more complex emotive and human forms or whether our ultimate satisfaction in other sculpture depends on the existence in it of her ultimate elements.

By reducing traditional forms of sculpture it is possible to see the geometry which underlies it and which is so obscure in more elaborate work. In the hands of Miss Hepworth this geometry has taken on particularly subtle form. At first sight there has been a great loss of complexity when compared with her earlier work. The negative curvatures and the twists have all but disappeared and we are treated to a series of surfaces of slightly varying positive curvature which enable the effects of small changes to be seen in a way that is impossible when the eye is distracted by grosser irregularities. The elements used are extremely simple : the sphere and the ellipsoid, the hollow cylinder and the hollow hemisphere. All the effects are gained either by slightly modulating these forms without breaking up their continuity, or by compositions combining two or three of them in different significant ways. The whole exhibition can be classified on the basis of these forms and of their combinations.

Five pieces show single forms (1, 15, 16, 18, 20) ; one is a subtly deformed sphere, the others, which we may call the four Menhirs though each has its distinctive individuality, gain immensely from being studied together. Though at first sight similar, comparison brings out subtle differences of entasis and change of section. They may indeed be considered to introduce a fourth dimension into sculpture, representing by a surface the movement of a closed curve in time. Nine other figures, three pierres percées (12, 14, 17), three cup and stone (6, 8, 11) and three cup and bar (4, 10, 13), bring out the theme of complementary forms, each solid structure being contrasted sharply with a hollow smaller, or larger, than itself. To this class also belongs the monumental stela (7) with its almost Peruvian emphasis on superposed rectangles.

Finally, six pieces (2, 3, 9, 19, 21, 23) bring out the relationship of similar figures, beginning with simple spheres and turning into discs and slabs of increasing complexity. Here the greatest thought has been given to exact placing

and orientation. There is not, as in representational art, any literary relation between the two pieces, or, as in architecture, any functional relation. The separate surfaces are made to belong to one another by virtue of their curvatures and their precise distances apart much as two sheets of a geometrically defined single surface.

The analysis is not complete without a consideration of the nature of the surfaces themselves. Material and finish have been as much thought out as geometric shape. The different uses of the various hard woods and marbles employed show that each surface has been thought of in relation to a material. This is particularly shown in the difference of the forms used for the hard and soft woods, emphasising very much the straight and twisted grain.

The historic associations and geometric significance of Miss Hepworth's work both raise the question of its general significance at the present time now that the particular form that art takes is becoming a matter of acute controversy and even an affair of state. Such abstract works as we have here can plainly not exist in a vacuum. They call for some form of social utilisation. Megalithic art was not aesthetic in intention, it represented the centre of a ritual which must have been so important in its time as to absorb the greater part of the free energies of its creators. If such art is to be of use now it needs to find the same public setting. Its geometrical character does in fact bring it immediately in relation with the developments of modern architecture. Its forms require to be combined integrally with those of buildings to which they would give a completeness that is at present lacking. So far this integration has not taken place, but one step to it might be the use of such pieces as are shown here in modern domestic architecture and it is to be hoped that the present exhibition will lead to an appreciation of this possibility.

Naum Gabo came over and decided to remain in England. Later Piet Mondrian also came and we found him a studio opposite our own.

Gropius, Moholy-Nagy, Breuer, Mendelssohn, had all come to live in London, and suddenly England seemed alive and rich – the centre of an international movement in architecture and art. We all seemed to be carried on the crest of this robust and inspiring wave of imaginative and creative energy. We were not at that time prepared to admit that it was a movement in flight. But because of the danger of totalitarianism and impending war, all of us worked the harder to lay strong foundations for the future through an understanding of the true relationship between architecture, painting, and sculpture.

Early in 1935 the idea of publishing a book on Constructive Art was born during an evening's conversation in our studio between J. L. Martin, Ben Nicholson, Naum Gabo, Sadie Speaight (Martin's wife), and myself. Work began on it almost at once.

95 *Pierced Hemisphere 1,* white marble,
14 in. (coll. Wakefield City Art Gallery).

97 My double-view photograph of *Two forms*

96 *Two forms* 1937, white marble, 26 in. (coll. Simon Nicholson).

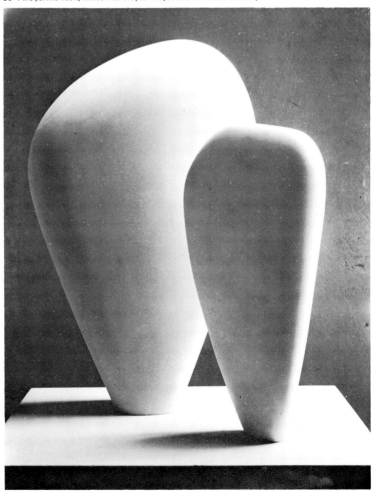

CIRCLE

EDITORS: J. L. MARTIN   BEN NICHOLSON   N. GABO

PAINTERS	SCULPTORS	ARCHITECTS	WRITERS
arp	brancusi	aalto	bernal
braque	calder	breuer	breuer
dacre	gabo	brinkman	corbusier
domela	giacometti	chermayeff	dacre
duchamp	hepworth	corbusier	fry
erni	holding	fischer	gabo
gris	meduniezky	fry	giedion
helion	moore	gropius	gropius
jackson	pevsner	havlíček	hepworth
kandinsky	tatlin	honzig	honzig
klee		jeanneret	martin
leger		loghem	massine
lissitzky		lubetkin	moholy-nagy
malevich		maillart	mondrian
moholy-nagy		martin	mumford
mondrian		mendelsohn	neutra
nicholson		molnar	read
picasso		nelson	richards
piper		neutra	sartoris
stephenson		nicholson	shand
taeuber-arp		praesens	tschichold
vordemberge		roth	
		roth	
		sartoris	
		syrkus	
		syrkus	
		tecton	
		vlugt	
		yorke	

FABER AND FABER

SCULPTURE
By Barbara Hepworth

I

FULL sculptural expression is spatial—it is the three-dimensional realization of an idea, either by mass or by space construction. The materials for sculpture are unlimited in their variety of quality, tenseness and aliveness. But for the imaginative idea to be fully and freely projected into stone, wood or any plastic substance, a complete sensibility to material—an understanding of its inherent quality and character—is required. There must be a perfect unity between the idea, the substance and the dimension : this unity gives scale. The idea—the imaginative concept—actually *is* the giving of life and vitality to material ; but when we come to define these qualities we find that they have very little to do with the physical aspect of the sculpture. When we say that a great sculpture has vision, power, vitality, scale, poise, form or beauty, we are not speaking of physical attributes. Vitality is not a physical, organic attribute of sculpture—it is a spiritual inner life. Power is not man power or physical capacity—it is an inner force and energy. Form realization is not just any three-dimensional mass—it is the chosen perfected form, of perfect size and shape, for the sculptural embodiment of the idea. Vision is not sight—it is the perception of the mind. It is the discernment of the reality of life, a piercing of the superficial surfaces of material existence, that gives to art its own life and purpose and significant power.

One of the most profound qualities of sculpture is scale—it can only be perceived intuitively because it is entirely a quality of thought and vision. Sculpture does not gain or lose spiritual significance by having more or less of physical attributes. A vital work has perfect co-ordination between conception and realization; but actual physical contours do not limit a perfected idea.

It does not matter whether a sculpture is asymmetrical or symmetrical—it

H   113

98 Cover of *Circle* published 1937, (99) my
article in *Circle* page 113 and (100) pages 114 and 115.

SCULPTURE

does not lose or gain by being either; for instance, it can be said that an asymmetrical sculpture has more points of view. But this is only one aspect of the sculptural entity—asymmetry can be found in the tension, balance, inner vital impact with space and in the scale.

The fact that a plastic projection of thought can only live by its inner power and not by physical content, means that the range for its choice of form is free and unlimited—the range of many forms to one form, surprising depths and juxtapositions to the most subtle, very small to very large. All are equal, and capable of the maximum of life according to the intensity of the vision.

Scale is not physical size, because a very small thing can have good scale or a very large thing poor scale—though often large sculptures achieve good scale because the artist approaches their conception with a greater seriousness and thought. Size can be emphasized by the juxtaposition of the very large to the very small; but this is only one side of sculptural relationships. There is the sculpture which has magnificent scale because of its precise and exact relationship between dimension and idea—it creates space for itself by its own vitality. There are two main sculptural identities—one which comes within the embrace of our hands and arms, and the other which stands free and unrelated to our sense of touch. Both have their distinct and individual quality of scale which makes an expansion and spaciousness in everything surrounding them. Scale is connected with our whole life—perhaps it is even our whole intuitive capacity to feel life.

II

The most difficult and complicated form relationships do not necessarily give a sculpture the fullest spiritual content. Very often, as the thought becomes more free the line is purified, and as principles—the laws which contain lesser laws—are comprehended, the forms become simplified and strengthened. In the physical world we can discover in the endless variations of the same form, the one particular form which demonstrates the power and robustness of the simplified structure—the form is clear and every part of it in precise unity with the whole. It is not the accidental or casual, but the regular irregularity, the perfect sequence which gives the maximum expression of individual life. In the three-dimensional realization there is always this exact form, or sequence of form—which can most fully and freely convey the idea. But there is no formula that can reveal the sequence; the premise is individual and the logical sequence purely intuitive—the result of equilibrium between thought and medium.

114

SCULPTURE

The perception of these differences, imperfections and perfections help us to understand the language the sculptor uses to convey the whole feeling and thought of his experience. It is the sculptor's work fully to comprehend the world of space and form, to project his individual understanding of his own life and time as it is related universally in this particular plastic extension of thought, and to keep alive this special side of existence. A clear social solution can only be achieved when there is a full consciousness in the realm of thought and when every section constitutes an inherent part of the whole.

The sculptural elements have long been neglected and unconsidered, the form consciousness of people has become atrophied; but now much is being done by a more balanced and free education—a greater co-ordination between hand and head—that will keep alive the intuitive form perceptions of the child. A world without form consciousness would scarcely be alive at all. The consciousness and understanding of volume and mass, laws of gravity, contour of the earth under our feet, thrusts and stresses of internal structure, space displacement and space volume, the relation of man to a mountain and man's eye to the horizon, and all laws of movement and equilibrium—these are surely the very essence of life, the principles and laws which are the vitalization of our experience, and sculpture a vehicle for projecting our sensibility to the whole of existence.

III

The whole life force is in the vision which includes all phantasy, all intuitive imagination, and all conscious selection from experience. Ideas are born through a perfect balance of our conscious and unconscious life and they are realized through this same fusion and equilibrium. The choice of one idea from several, and the capacity to relate the whole of our past experience to the present idea is our conscious mind: our sensitivity to the unfolding of the idea in substance, in relation to the very act of breathing, is our unconscious intuition.

'Abstract' is a word which is now most frequently used to express only the type of the outer form of a work of art; this makes it difficult to use it in relation to the spiritual vitality or inner life which is the real sculpture. Abstract sculptural qualities are found in good sculpture of all time, but it is significant that contemporary sculpture and painting have become abstract in thought and concept. As the sculptural idea is in itself unfettered and unlimited and can choose its own forms, the vital concept selects the form and substance of its expression quite unconsciously.

115

38

BARBARA HEPWORTH

CONSTRUCTIVIST

Born 1903 at Wakefield, Yorkshire. Studied at Leeds School of Art, Royal College of Art, in Florence and Rome; member of "Unit One" 1933, "Abstraction-Creation" group 1933-34 and "Seven and Five" Society 1930-1936.

102 Simon

Helicoids in Sphere (1938), Teak

101 With *Helicoids in Sphere* from 'Living Art in England'

103 Rachel

My own work went well. Carving became increasingly rhythmical, and I was aware of the special pleasure that sculptors can have through carving, that of a complete unity of physical and mental rhythm. It seemed to be the most natural occupation in the world. It is perhaps strange that I should have become aware of this at the moment when the forms themselves had become the absolute reverse of all that was arbitary — when there had developed a deliberate conception of form and relationship.

The children prospered and grew and laughed. They had a terrific sense of fun. The red-letter days were when Gabo or Calder, and later, Mondrian, came to share nursery tea. Three pairs of eyes would watch every movement, and three pairs of ears listen to every word.

Circle was published at last. Mondrain had made his studio opposite so very beautiful, and his company was always inspiring, as it had been in Paris when we used to visit him. After a while he really seemed to enjoy our domestic scene. His studio and Ben's were most austere, but my studio was a jumble of children, rocks, sculptures, trees, importunate flowers and washing.

104 Sarah

105 *Forms and Hollows*, plaster, 10 in.

106 *Project for sculpture in a landscape*, plaster, 18 in. (Destroyed in war)

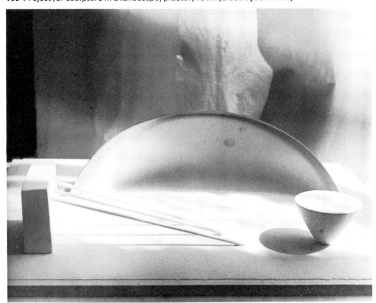

107 Adrian Stokes

108 *Project for garden sculpture*, plaster, 12 in.

109 *Sculpture with colour,*
white, blue and red strings, 10 in.

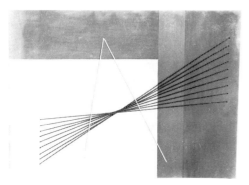

110 *Construction*, 1938, on board with
string and colour, 20 x 14 in.

1938 to 1939 were the years of attrition. It became harder and harder to sell any work or get jobs of any kind. Lacking money, space and time, I became obsessed by ideas for large works. I had, between 1934 and 1937, achieved three large works over 10 feet high (all damaged during the war), but now, for the first time I had to work imaginatively in maquette form and dream up some future monument.

These maquettes were all lost in the war years; but I had photographed them, and bided my time until many years later money, and space and time could be found.

I love working on a large scale so that the whole body of the spectator becomes involved. I also had an obsession about colour in the concavities of forms. The latter I realized more fully in the years between 1943 1946.

Adrian Stokes, who by then had a beautiful house in Carbis Bay, invited all of us for a holiday; and, he added, if war broke out he would give shelter to the children, as a glass-roofed studio in London was no place for them. For about four months he and his wife gave us shelter, warmth and kindness until we found a way to live.

Ben knew St. Ives; but in spite of what Prof. J. D. Bernal wrote (prophetically) in 1937, I felt opposed to coming to a place I had never seen. Arriving in August at midnight with very weary children, in pouring rain, my spirits were at zero. Next morning I appreciated the beauty and the sense of community, and realised that it would be possible to find some manual work and raise the children, and take part in community life, which has nourished me ever since. Soon after, Naum Gabo and his wife Miriam arrived. War had been declared, and we set about finding ways of working and helping the war effort.

The last person we saw in August was Mondrian, and we begged him to come with us in our battered old car (which we bought for £17) so that we could look after him. But he would not.

111 Miriam and Naum Gabo

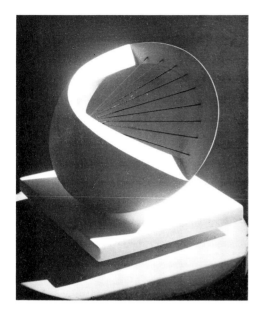

Here I must pay the greatest possible tribute to *Adrian Stokes our life-long friend. His generous help and encouragement made the first three years of the war just supportable.*

I could only draw at night and make a few plaster maquettes. The day was filled with running a nursery school, double-cropping a tiny garden for food, and trying to feed and protect the children. I did not resent the war effort or the hard work, but I did begin to worry about the future: we were picking our salads in the hedgerows, and mushrooms in the fields, while the children's appetites grew bigger and bigger.

112 (above, left) *Sculpture with colour and strings*, 1940, plaster, 4 in.

113 Alfred Wallis in 1941

114 (below left) The Nursery School

115 Paul

116 *Porthmeor Square and Island* by Alfred Wallis

117 Simon, Rachel and Sarah

118 *Drawing for sculpture,* gouache and pencil, 9½ x 14 in. (coll. John Wells).

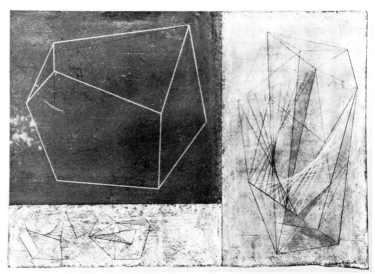

NEW MOVEMENTS IN ART
CONTEMPORARY WORK
IN ENGLAND

AN EXHIBITION OF RECENT

PAINTING AND SCULPTURE

MARCH 18 - MAY 9 *1942*
LONDON MUSEUM
LANCASTER HOUSE S.W.1

119 Catalogue cover of 'New
Movements in Art' Exhibition

120 'New Movements in Art' Exhibition at the London Museum

Temple Newsam
Leeds

PAUL NASH

BARBARA
HEPWORTH

24 April—13 June
1943

6ᵈ·

121 Catalogue cover of Exhibition
at Temple Newsam, Leeds

606   THE LISTENER   20 MAY 1943

Modern Art at Temple Newsam

By WILLIAM GIBSON

TEMPLE NEWSAM was acquired by Leeds in 1922, and the interior has been redecorated by Professor Hendy in a series of rooms beautifully furnished in late seventeenth- and eighteenth-century styles, together with a suite of galleries for exhibitions. The exhibitions are to be regarded as part of this whole. Since the other rooms are arranged as living rooms, one sees the exhibitions much as one sees works of art in one's own home. The gain is enormous — one sees the things comfortably and without fuss. Mixing the study of pictures and sculpture with the enjoyment of beautiful rooms, one is free from the all too usual battle between the attraction of the exhibits and the repulsion of their surroundings; and this effect is increased by the absence of top-lighting, perhaps the deadliest weapon in the whole philistine armoury of the traditional picture gallery. Coming to the exhibition after looking at such things as chairs, mirrors and porcelain, which no one has difficulty in understanding, one is less likely to make difficulties for oneself about a novel form of art by assuming difficulties to exist. Finally, visiting the exhibition galleries as part of a furnished house, not of a museum, one tends naturally to look at pictures and sculpture as works of art, not as material for classification and historical study.

It is interesting and at the same time satisfying, however cheaply, to those who have come to understand and admire Miss Hepworth's mature work on its own merits, to see in this exhibition the long period of personal experience and practical experiment by which it has been evolved. If, moreover, this satisfaction is rather of tinsel than of the genuine article, if it has something of the ignoble 'told you so' about it, we are at least with a clear conscience in the position to appreciate and enjoy the adventures through which she has been. These adventures, productive though they were of much beautiful and expressive work, can only be described in the short space available as earlier essays in representing carving under a number of varying influences, and later essays in the semi-abstract under the influence of Mr. Henry Moore, or possibly of such continental sculptors as M. Arp, out of which the sculptress ultimately finds her own individuality in purely unrepresentational and chiefly geometric forms. She has stripped her art of all associational appeal and found herself in a world of related plastic shapes, of contrasting and harmonizing curves, and of tensions of arrested movement. How much is inspired by the actual visible world I cannot say, and to the mind accustomed to the more complex forms of traditional sculpture her simple shapes may at first sight seem lacking both in form and matter. But as one becomes acquainted with one of them, one senses its distinct individuality, and as one feels one's way imaginatively over and into the objects (? hence the introduction of holes), the experience grows of the interplay of force, of movement and of tension, latent, as it were, in the lines of the individual objects, in the intervals between them, and in the relationship of their shapes, one to another (e.g. of the sphere to the hollow in the carving

'Convoid, Sphere and Hollow' (white marble) 1937, by Barbara Hepworth. From the collection of Alastair Morton

reproduced). One exhibit, No. 110, severely geometrical, is coloured and includes the use of string : the first version was made in 1941, and it seems to mark a new development. It is wise to express no opinion at this stage. This, however, should be said : Miss Hepworth has, I understand, made few carvings recently ; both her previous sculpture and the increasing beauty of her drawings, many of which are shewn, make it fervently to be hoped that she will soon provide full opportunity of studying the newer style. If this is a period of gestation, good and well. Miss Hepworth, as we have seen, is an artist who develops her art slowly after considerable private experience and cogitation. If, on the other hand, it is the result of external circumstance, it is a tragedy, for there is no doubt that her work is a permanent contribution to the art of sculpture.

In contrast with Miss Hepworth, Mr. Nash found a personal style almost at once. This is largely true of the earliest drawings here (1913, 1918) ; and in the earliest works in which a definite style is established (those made at Dymchurch from 1923 onwards), there is little to connect him with others except the concentration on design which he shares with the better artists of his own and the preceding generations. This is one of his greatest virtues. The choice for the English painter is so often put as between two alternatives. He must either, it is implied, make pastiches after a continental model, or, the right course, he must abandon construction and design, the backbone of all great traditions of painting, for a vague literary poeticism, facetiousness or what not, which is assumed to be proper to his native talents. Mr. Nash has refused to agree that the English painter cannot be a painter in the grand tradition. He has been undeterred from concerning himself with the essential business of the artist, the organisation of space, and at the same time he has resisted the temptation to become a mere imitator of the superficial aspects, the fashions, of continental painting. As a result he is one of the few artists of essential importance in English painting today.

The contrast with the older styles in the rest of the house is one of the advantages of holding modern exhibitions at Temple Newsam and is given an added force in the present instance by reason of a certain similarity between the forms employed by the two artists which gives a pronounced decorative unity to the galleries in which they are shewn. To enter these after experiencing the emphatic rhythms of the great saloon with its magnificent rococo mirrors, wall-lights and tables and boldly coloured needlework chairs, is to be vividly aware of the rhythm of the modern work. Everyone with a liking for modern art must frequently have met with the request 'I can't understand it. Do explain it to me' on the part of someone genuinely open-minded. The trouble, of course, is that it is not a matter of understanding in the sense of comprehending, but of experiencing and enjoying visually. If one has felt the rhythm of modern works, one is at least well on the way to understanding them.

122 Article on Modern Art at
Temple Newsam by W. Gibson

Mercifully, by 1943 we found a large and very shabby old house at Carbis Bay. This was wonderful – it gave Ben a reasonable studio, one for me near the kitchen, and room for the children. It was rough, but roomy for a growing family and gave Ben some rest, after being out all night on Home-Guard, from the noise of family life.

Our work began to flow again and the children were growing. Soon we realised that they were nearly ten years old and would have to go free. They could no longer be told to carry gas masks and not touch anything, or be oppressed by 'No', 'No', and 'No'.

And looking back, I must say how good Leonard and Dorothy Elmhirst were to us. We had, of course, met in the 1930's when Mark Tobey was working at Darlington Hall, and Gropius came with us on a visit there. But the scholarships they gave for the children meant so much. The children grew and thrived there. I remember the Headmaster, William Curry, saying 'Twins have been a lot of bother – but I am quite prepared to see what happens with triplets.' We owe so much to Dartington Hall.

123 Naum Gabo and his daughter

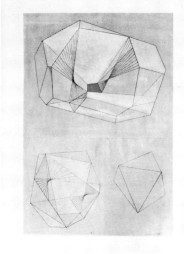

124 Frontispiece *Crystal* 1942 and title page of *Stone and Flower*

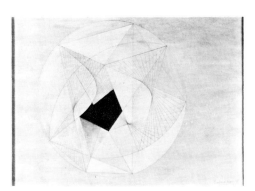

125 *Circle*, gouache and pencil, 15 x 20¼ in. (coll. E. H. Ramsden and Margot Eates).

126 Simon, Rachel, Sarah and Paul at Carbis Bay

127 Ben at Carbis Bay

129 At Carbis Bay

128 Elizabeth and John Summerson

130 Naum Gabo and his dog

131 Foreword by Herbert Read of catalogue of Bankfield Museum Exhibition

132 Catalogue cover of Bankfield
Museum Exhibition, Halifax

BARBARA HEPWORTH

The past fifty years has seen a remarkable revival of the art of sculpture, which since the Renaissance had sunk so low that it had lost all its essential meaning. We might say that the art which the great epochs of the ancient World and of the Middle Ages chose for the vehicle of their highest conceptions of truth and beauty had become a rival to the waxworks exhibition. From that state it was rescued by great artists like Rodin and Maillol and slowly, from the new foundations they laid, the art of sculpture has been re-established to its former significance and dignity. To the latest stages of this historical process two Yorkshire sculptors, Barbara Hepworth and Henry Moore, have made decisive contributions. Yorkshire ought to be proud of that fact, and not be slow in paying its tribute to the genius which has sprung from its soil and which the wide world is beginning to acclaim.

It is particularly appropriate that an exhibition of Barbara Hepworth's work should be held in Wakefield, for she was born in that city and educated at its Girl's High School. Her studies were continued with the aid of county scholarships at Leeds School of Art and the Royal College of Art, and in 1924-5 she completed these studies in Italy with the aid of a West Riding Scholarship Grant. She had her first exhibition at the Beaux Arts Gallery in London in 1929, followed by exhibitions at Tooth's Gallery in 1930 and 1932 and at the Lefevre Galleries in 1933 and 1937. She has contributed to various exhibitions in London, Paris and Amsterdam in the past ten years, and her work is represented in the Museum of Modern Art, New York, in the Manchester and Wakefield Art Galleries, and at Temple Newsam, Leeds.

The present exhibition shows the evolution of Barbara Hepworth's art from 1929 onwards, and demands from the visitor, who would understand the aims of the artist and appreciate the beauty of her achievements, something more than the cursory glance which is given to conventional pictures and statues. The artist is not trying to " imitate " anything—so much, it may be said, is obvious. But what does the conventional artist imitate ' He would answer " Nature ", meaning by that term the visual impressions he receives from the apparent surfaces of things. But we all know that appearance is not necessarily reality, and that beneath all the changes which our senses record there is a permanent structure which is far more essential to an understanding of life or the universe. We might say that the aim of

an artist like Barbara Hepworth is to give us some understanding of this essential structure. That, of course, is also the aim of modern science, but science works by reason, analysis, dissection, classification—a necessary method in which, however, the essential wholeness of phenomena is destroyed. The artist, on the other hand, works by intuition, synthesis, insight and sympathy, and is thus able to give some account of the essential wholeness which underlies the shifting appearances of nature. So, after all, this modern art is an " imitation " of something. Better still, it is a translation of something—a translation of intuitions and perceptions of the nature of reality into permanent materials like wood, stone and metal. In the process of translation a compromise must be made, because these materials have their own " natural " laws, and the nature of an impermanent material like flesh cannot be directly translated into the terms of a permanent material like stone without submitting to what is superficially a distortion, but which is essentially an exactness or fidelity of representation.

There is one further stage or process which a constructive artist like Barbara Hepworth has taken, and which explains her latest work. Once a form is taken from nature—and it may be taken from the properties of crystals as well as from the properties of flowers or human figures—then the " theme " so selected can be developed into a series of " variations ", strictly comparable to the variations which a composer makes on a musical theme. The form which the sculptor may finally select for representation in the solid substance of wood or stone may have been mentally evolved from an earlier form taken directly from nature. In art it is the life of forms that matters, not the form of life.

That is about as much as can be said in a brief and necessarily concentrated Foreword, but I shall have failed in my purpose if I have given the impression that the art of Barbara Hepworth must be approached with a thinking-cap on. Art should first be loved, and then explained. Barbara Hepworth's carvings and drawings live in their beauty, and all they ask is the simple sensuous reception we would give to a flower or a shell, or the lovely pebble we instinctively pick up from the beach.

HERBERT READ

EXHIBITION OF
SCULPTURE AND
DRAWINGS BY
BARBARA HEPWORTH

BANKFIELD
MUSEUM
HALIFAX

MARCH 18th —
APRIL 15th 1944

CATALOGUE
SIXPENCE

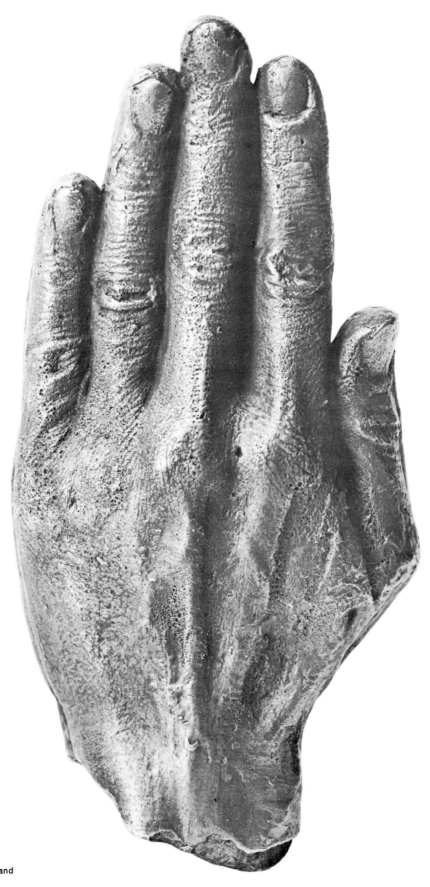

133 Cast of left hand by my right hand

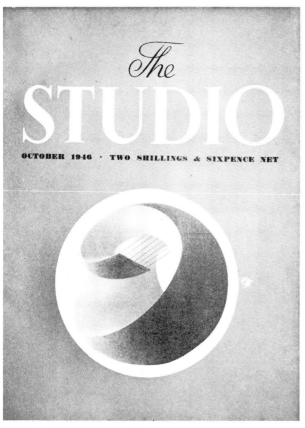

Miss Hepworth answers questions, put to her by the Editor, on her work, which will be on view during October at the Reid and Lefèvre Galleries.

a p p r o a c h   t o
SCULPTURE

BY BARBARA HEPWORTH

ARE you self-taught, or have you had tuition? If so, by whom?

I was at Leeds School of Art for one year and the Royal College of Art for three years, on County Scholarships; at the end of this time I went to Italy as a travelling scholarship.

Direct carving was not a definite part of the curriculum at that time; but I feel that with carving, as with painting, the craft has to be rediscovered by each artist afresh, and that technique is just the outcome of this particular and very personal discovery.

I was a child to an Italian master-carver, Ardini, whose remarks on the approach to marble carving, when I was in Rome, opened up a new vista for me of the quality of form, light, and colour contained in the Mediterranean conception of carving.

The great virtue of an Art School lies in the opportunity it gives to the student to work with his contemporaries, to be provided with models, props, etc. means to have live materials to experiment with, and museums to study sculpture and drawings, but tuition should be a kind of collective instrument so that every student can exercise his own faculties in the sense of discovery. Unfortunately so many students are repelled in the first approach to painting and carving in schools for a long time because such an Art School, because of the past limitations of the qualities necessary to a good art teacher.

Whose of the world's sculpture do you most admire?

I cannot really answer this question in a direct way. When I think of the many great cultures of the past it becomes impossible to think of any one sculptor, or any one sculpture – the richness and diversity is so great. But thinking contemporaneously it is possible to see the continuity in direct line with the past – the real sculptural principles kept alive by a few sculptors in Europe – and to feel sad that world conditions, abstract and obscure, a reawakened understanding of architecture and sculpture.

Has your preference always been for abstract form?

No – my work was representational at first and has gradually become more and more abstract.

For how long have you been interested in, may I say, "Ovoid" shapes as a basis for sculptured form?

I have always been interested in oval or ovoid shapes. The first carvings were simple realistic oval forms of the human head or of a bird. Gradually my interest grew in more abstract values – the weight,

97

BARBARA HEPWORTH. *ELEGY* (BEECH wood) 1946. 15 INS. HIGH. *Below:* TWO FIGURES (REDWOOD) 1943. 27 INS. HIGH

134 Cover of *The Studio* Illus. *Pelagos*

135 (top right) My article in *The Studio* October 1946

136 'Approach to Sculpture' pages 98 and 99, and (137) pages 100 and 101

138 Catalogue cover of Lefevre Gallery Exhibition

BARBARA HEPWORTH

sculpture and drawings

OCTOBER 1946

THE   LEFEVRE   GALLERY
(ALEX REID & LEFEVRE, LTD.)
131-134 NEW BOND STREET
LONDON, W.1

ILLUSTRATED CATALOGUE   PRICE SIXPENCE

136

137

139 Book jacket, 1946

ARIEL BOOKS ON THE ARTS

Barbara Hepworth

INTRODUCTION BY WILLIAM GIBSON

PUBLISHED FOR THE SHENVAL PRESS
BY FABER AND FABER LIMITED

140 Article by E. H. Ramsden in *Polemic*

At Carbis Bay, during the mid-forties, I did some of my best work. I had only limited space: a back-yard, a room only eight feet high, and endless complaints about my hammering! The sound of a mallet or hammer is music to my ears, when either is used rhythmically, and I can tell by sound alone what is going on; but I could understand how exasperating this could be to neighbours and indeed to the family. Ben needed a really good big studio and this was more easily obtained for a painter than a sculptor. All these later years in the 1940's we were in close touch with our oldest friends, who came to stay down here: Herbert and Ludo Read, Solly Zuckerman and his wife Joan, Professor J. D. Bernal, my sister Elizabeth and John Summerson, our friends Marcus and Rene Brumwell, Peter Gregory and Margaret Gardiner and many others joined us from time to time. With their help, and the nucleus in St. Ives of Naum and Miriam Gabo, Adrian Stokes, Bernard Leach and Peter Lanyon, the Penwith Society of Arts was born.

Throughout the two decades our great hopes were being realised and aided by our friendship with Duncan Macdonald and his wife Lily, who had the utmost faith in our work, although this faith gave them no financial reward whatsoever. His death, shortly after one of my post-war exhibitions, really shattered me, because we were still so very hard-up and it seemed as though our friend and mentor had left us totally bereft. What I did not perceive at this time, either because I was too tired or too stupid, or both, was that the house was cracking up and the family bursting at the seams.

Three children of the same age want everything at the same time; but individually. This was a problem for them as well as for Ben and me. It is a good thing, perhaps, that one does not foresee tragedy ahead.

In 1951, after twenty years of family life, everything was to fall apart.

Page 33

E. H. Ramsden

THE SCULPTURE OF BARBARA HEPWORTH

The process of transformation—even that of the visible into the invisible which Rainer Maria Rilke proclaimed as an historical necessity of our time and celebrated in the Duino Elegies with all the fervour of which he was capable, is that of which the artist, above all others, is most profoundly aware. But while to recreate the patterns of experience in terms which become progressively more evanescent is for the poet sufficiently arduous a task, for the sculptor who finds himself similarly impelled the problems involved are immeasurably more complex, more formidable and more austere, since to him belongs the necessity of giving tangible shape to ideas and intuitions which ordinarily transcend the limits of the concrete and have hitherto remained beyond the aspirations of artistic faith.

Under these circumstances should the sculptor no longer seek to express his emotional reactions to the visible forms of the world through the imitative methods proper to an earlier generation, this is due not to caprice, but to an instinctive recognition that such methods are wholly irrelevant to his purpose—largely perhaps because it is no longer in the isolated form of an existence that Nature survives for him but in the sublimated form of an event. Similarly, no longer is it towards the constants but towards the variables in all fields of activity that attention is now directed. In the sciences it is the notion not of substance but of function that is operative; in the arts not the circumscribed 'thing' but the 'imageless act' of an intensified experience that pervades the soul. There is a deepening conviction, in other words, that it is the modes of the interconnectedness of things rather than the things themselves, the evolving curve rather than the completed figure, the process of 'becoming' rather than the state of 'become' that is ultimately significant. It is therefore inevitable that this consciousness of the *in betweenness* of things, this passionate sense that:

Between the hammers lives on
our heart, as between the teeth
the tongue . . . .

should find expression in plastic art under new and ever more subtle

In 1947 it was suggested to me that I might be interested in watching an operation in a hospital. At first I was very scared, but then I found there was such beauty in the co-ordinated human endeavour in the operating theatre that the whole composition – human in appearance – became abstract in shape. I became completely absorbed by two things: first, the extraordinary beauty of purpose between human beings all dedicated to the saving of life; and secondly by the way this special grace (grace of mind and body) induced a spontaneous space composition, an articulated and animated kind of abstract sculpture very close to what I had been seeking in my own work. I wasn't trying to tell a story, but the experience proved a theory I had – that no matter how many people involved – their action and poise and intention produced drawings rather like a ballet; though the ballet is contrived, whereas in the operating theatre the action is not contrived but disciplined and at the same time intuitive. In a fearful emergency everybody goes into the

Colour and 'form' go hand in hand –
brown fields & green hills cannot
be divorced from the earth's shape –
a square becomes a triangle,
a triangle a circle, a circle an oval
by the continuous curve of folding:
and we return, always, to the
essential human form – the human
form in landscape

Barbara Hepworth
June 1947

50

*right sort of place, and the most extra-
ordinary shapes are made.*

*A particularly beautiful example of the
difference between physical and spiritual
animation can be observed in a delicate
operation on the human hand. There you have
the inanimate hand asleep and the active,
conscious hand: the relation of these two was
so beautiful it made me look in a new light
at human faces, hands when people are talking, at the way a tree grows, and a flower.*

PAINTINGS BY

BARBARA HEPWORTH

PAINTINGS BY

L. S. LOWRY

APRIL, 1948

THE LEFEVRE GALLERY

Alex. Reid & Lefevre Ltd.

131-134 NEW BOND STREET
LONDON, W.1

143 Catalogue cover of
Lefevre Gallery Exhibition

---

592   THE LISTENER   APRIL 8 1948

Barbara Hepworth: a New Phase

By HERBERT READ

BARBARA HEPWORTH is well known as a sculptor whose work, during the past fifteen years, has developed to a purity of 'abstraction' which has seemed to the casual observer to bring her into close relationship with the geometry of solid figures. That the formal elements in art can be explained in accordance with definite laws of number or proportion was well known to the Greeks, and perhaps even earlier to the Egyptians, and Plato considered the possibility of an art based on these laws, rather than on the direct imitation of nature. At various periods in the history of art, artists have altogether abandoned representational realism, perhaps because they felt that the world was too much with them (as it may have been in the New Stone Age or in the age of the Vikings), or because they felt there was some impiety involved in the imitation of God's creation (as in the Islamic or Arabic civilisation). But it is only in modern times that a non-representational type of art has been developed as a separate and self-consistent style, challenging comparison with other contemporary styles (realism, impressionism, expressionism, surrealism, etc.). This new movement is popularly known as 'abstract' art, by which we mean an art derived or disengaged from nature, the pure or essential form abstracted from the concrete details. The term is not very satisfactory, and several alternatives have been suggested and even adopted by particular schools within this movement (synthetic cubism, neo-plasticism, constructivism, suprematism, etc.), but these labels often indicate a distinct aim (constructivism, for example, disclaiming any relationship to nature, even to the formal structure of matter or the forms assumed by vital organisms), and the general terms, realism and abstraction, serve best to indicate the two extremes of expression in art.

There are abstract artists of dogmatic austerity who would never deviate from their practice of an art of pure form—the Dutch painter, Piet Mondrian, is an example. And there are, of course, many realistic artists who would never dream of painting abstract compositions. There have been abstract artists who have renounced their abstract aims and returned to realistic art; and there have been realistic artists of considerable talent who have suddenly renounced their realism and taken to abstraction. Another group, however, has seen no reason why it should not alternate between the two styles, and it is to this group that Barbara Hepworth now belongs.

Her earliest work (1929-32) was naturalistic—based, for the most part, on a close observation of the human figure. Some of these early carvings are of great beauty, but the emphasis on the purely formal elements increases gradually, until finally complete freedom from the model is achieved, and all reference to natural objects is abandoned (the titles, for example, become 'forms', 'discs', 'spheres', 'conicoids', instead of 'mother and child', etc.). The carvings and drawings shown at an exhibition of her work held in the Lefevre Galleries in October 1946 were almost exclusively of this nature. Now, eighteen months later, the same galleries are showing an exhibition of her work which is predominantly realistic. What is surprising about the work in this ex-

'Pause', oil and pencil, 1948, by Barbara Hepworth

hibition, however, is not its realistic character, but its quite extraordinary depth of feeling. Barbara Hepworth has emerged from a phase of abstraction with her sympathy for natural forms greatly enhanced, her technique developed in power and subtlety, and, more surprisingly, a quality of realism of the most intense and dramatic kind.

The new paintings and drawings (many are executed in a technique which combines oil and pencil) fall into two groups—figure studies of the female nude, and hospital scenes. It is the latter which are so powerful and moving in their restraint and intensity. The hospital is, of course, a dramatic setting—we speak of the operating *theatre*, and it is generally from this theatre that Barbara Hepworth has taken her subjects. The pain and the fear are sublimated—absorbed in the creative purpose of the surgeon, gathered into his sensitive hands, into the patient faces of the nurses, who stand in the wings like a Greek chorus. Rembrandt and other Dutch painters were fond of such subjects, but it is not their type of realism of which we are reminded—rather of the austere humanism of the *Quattrocento* in Italy. There is a sense of monumental form which can only come to artists conscious of abstract form. The Italian artists were highly conscious of the abstract art of architecture. In the case of Barbara Hepworth (as in the parallel case of Henry Moore) the monumentality she achieves in her realistic figures is due to the practice of an art of pure form.

Abstract art (I exclude constructivism, which is another story) like realistic art, is always in danger of degenerating into academicism. It fails to renew its forces at the source of all forms, which is not so much nature as the vital impulses which determine the evolution of life itself. For that reason alone it may be suggested that an alternation between abstraction and realism is desirable in any artist. This does not mean that abstract art should be treated merely as a preparatory exercise for realistic art. Abstract art exists in its own rights. But the change-over from one style to another, from realism to abstraction and from abstraction to realism, need not be accompanied by any deep psychological process. It is merely a change of direction, of destination. What is constant is the desire to create a reality, a coherent world of vital images. At one extreme that 'will to form' is expressed in the creation of what might be called *free* images, so long as we do not assume that freedom implies any lack of aesthetic discipline; and at the other extreme the will to form is expressed in a selective affirmation of some aspect of the organic world—notably as a heightened awareness of the vitality or grace of the human figure. Some words of Barbara Hepworth's express this antithesis perfectly. 'Working realistically replenishes one's *love* for life, humanity and the earth. Working abstractly seems to release one's personality and sharpen the perceptions, so that in the observation of life it is the wholeness or inner intention which moves one so profoundly: the components fall into place, the detail is significant of unity.'

It is the whole scope of art itself that is illustrated by these two extremes which are now seen to lie within the capacity of a single mind

144 Article by Herbert Read in *The Listener*. Illus. *Pause*

---

145 *Concourse (2)* 48 x 30 in. (coll. The Royal College of Surgeons, London).

141 (opposite above) *Study*, red chalk,
13¾ x 9½ in. (coll. Dr Barlow).

142 (opposite) Statement

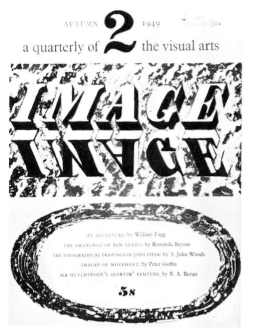

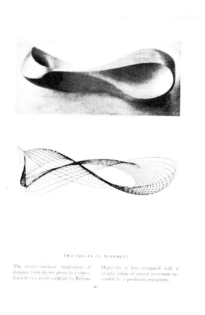

Finding Trewyn Studio was a sort of magic. For ten years I had passed by with my shopping bags not knowing what lay behind the twenty-foot walls. It was my friend Marcus Brumwell who persuaded me to go to the auction and bid for the place when it came up for sale.

Here was a studio, a yard and garden where I could work in open air and space. A friend accompanied me to the auction to bid for me and asked me what my bid was. I said 'I will stop you when it is beyond my figure'. The first bid was far beyond my figure and, according to my friends, I went pale green and fainted – so the bidding went on and I got the place. I was terrified; but Marcus said 'don't be silly – you have an ideal place, now get to work and you will be able to pay for it'. He was right. I was faint-hearted and there I was – space, air, sun and a real proper workshop. The children had their own quarters just opposite and Ben his own big studio, and we all began to expand and grow.

It was at this time that my friends Frank and Nancibel Halliday and their son Sebastian came into my life, in 1949. For twenty years Frank and Nancie have generously helped me to take on a position in life for which I was ill-equipped, that of being a sort of head of the family.

146 Cover of *Image* No.2, Autumn 1949

147 Article by Peter Goffin in *Image* No.2, page 60

148 My newly acquired Trewyn Studio

BARBARA HEPWORTH

October third through October twenty-ninth

149 Catalogue cover of Durlacher Bros. Exhibition, 1949

DURLACHER BROS.

11 East 57th Street

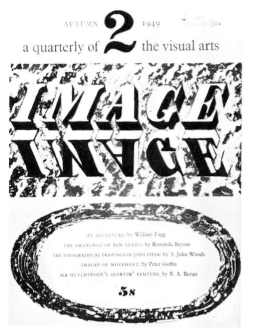

In sculpture there must be a complete realisation of the structure and quality of the stone or wood which is being carved. But I do not think that this alone supplies the life and vitality of sculpture. I believe that the understanding of the material and the meaning of the form being carved must be in perfect equilibrium. There are fundamental shapes which speak at all times and periods in the language of sculpture.

It is difficult to describe in words the meaning of forms because it is precisely this emotion which is conveyed by sculpture alone. Our sense of touch is a fundamental sensibility which comes into action at birth — our stereognostic sense — the ability to feel weight and form and assess its significance. The forms which have had special meaning for me since childhood have been the standing form (which is the translation of my feeling towards the human being standing in landscape); the two forms (which is the tender relationship of one living thing beside another); and the closed form, such as the oval, spherical or pierced form (sometimes incorporating colour) which translates for me the association and meaning of gesture in landscape; in the repose of say a mother and child, or the feeling of the embrace of living things, either in nature or in the human spirit. In all these shapes the translation of what one feels about man and nature must be conveyed by the sculptor in terms of mass, inner tension and rhythm, scale in relation to our human size and the quality of surface which speaks through our hands and eyes.

I think that the necessary equilibrium between the material I carve and the form I want to make will always dictate an abstract interpretation in my sculpture — for there are essential stone shapes and essential wood shapes which are impossible for me to disregard. All my feeling has to be translated into this basic framework, for sculpture is the reaction of a real object which relates to our human body and spirit as well as to our visual appreciation of form and colour content.

150 *Turning forms*, reinforced concrete, 84 in. Commissioned for The Festival of Britain

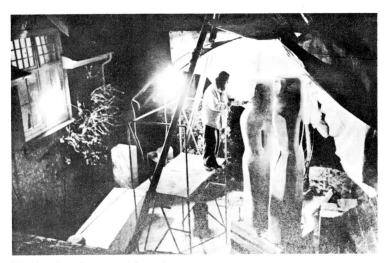

151 At work on *Contrapuntal forms*, 1950–51

For twenty-five years, walking through these streets, I have felt through my feet the geological shape of the place. The aerial view proved to me my point; it is through our senses that form, colour and meaning are given to everything we make and do. I wrote about St Ives many years ago: 'The sea, a flat diminishing plane, held within itself the capacity to radiate an infinitude of blues, greys, greens and even pinks of strange hues, the lighthouse and its strange rocky island was the eye: the Island of St Ives an arm, a hand, a face. The rock formation of the great bay had a withinness of form that led my imagination straight to the country of West Penwith behind me — although the visual thrust was straight out to sea. The incoming

153 'The pattern under our feet'

tolerated. And so one isn't an oddity, but just another chap rushing out in overalls to buy some more files at the nearest shop. St Ives has absolutely enraptured me, not merely for its beauty, but the naturalness of life — I love the way people will just stand in the way talking and laughing, they won't move. The sense of community is, I think, a very important factor in an artist's life.

154 (left) St Ives from the air showing Trewyn Studio amongst the trees in the centre

and receding tides made strange and wonderful calligraphy on the pale granite sand that sparkled with felspar and mica. The rich mineral deposits of Cornwall were apparent on the very surface of things; geology and prehistory — a thousand facts induced a thousand fantasies of form and purpose, structure and life which had gone into the making of what I saw and what I was.'

It is very difficult in cities to be aware of these marvellous happenings, which become very potent if one begins really living and putting down roots, and I am so fortunate here to have a garden and space and buildings where I can make such a mess and be

155 St Ives from the air

152 *Contrapuntal forms*, blue limestone, 120 in. Commissioned by the Arts Council for the Festival of Britain

BARBARA HEPWORTH
SCULPTURE AND DRAWINGS

1951 FESTIVAL OF BRITAIN
WAKEFIELD CITY ART GALLERY
MAY 19th — JULY 7th

156 Catalogue cover of Wakefield Exhibition

Working realistically replenishes one's love for life, humanity and the earth. Working abstractly seems to release one's personality and sharpen the perceptions, so that in the observation of life it is the wholeness or inner intention which moves one so profoundly: the components fall into place, the detail is significant of unity.

157 Venice — bird movement

158 Front page of Penwith Society of Arts 'Summer Broadsheet' with *Rock form (Penwith)*

159 Article by Kenneth Martin 'Abstract Art' in A.I.A. Gallery Broadsheet No.1

Some Questions of Patronage to-day

Winners at the Penwith Society's Festival Competition — Painting (W. Barns-Graham (left) with her "Cornish Landscape (Evening) Porthleven, 1951"; Sculpture : Barbara Hepworth (rt.) with her "Rock Form, Penwith (Portland Stone)1951"; centre, Bernard Leach's lidded pot. Judges : Mr. John Rothenstein (Tate Gallery), Mr. Philip James (Arts Council) and Ald. Gerald Cock. The prize-winning entries are to be presented to the Borough of St. Ives.

The Penwith Society receives an annual endowment from the Arts Council of Great Britain. The extent of this munificence does not amount to complete support. But it is the generous minimum which makes survival possible —at least from the point of view of running costs.

Over and above this, the Arts Council has supported the Society indirectly, by buying and commissioning works by some of its members. It has bought a large painting by W. Barns-Graham; it has commissioned work by a Penwith sculptor, the two vast *Contrapuntal Forms* by Barbara Hepworth in Irish blue limestone now to be seen outside the Dome of Discovery in the South Bank exhibition; it has included in its *60 Paintings for 51* exhibition three paintings of extra-easel proportions by members of the Penwith Society, Ben Nicholson, Patrick Heron, Bryan Winter, Victor Pasmore, and another by Peter Lanyon, an ex-member of the Society who lives in West Penwith; these, that

My first visit to Venice: and against the superb proportions of the buildings set in the expanded flatness of water, or confined, or rising out of ribboned canals where one is so aware of the magnitude of the sky, I watched new movements of people. The animation of light and shadow over earth colours of black, white, grey and red in the architecture was so vital in relation to the proportions of mass and space that every human action against this

161 *Biolith* 1948–9. Shown at 25th Venice Biennale and awarded Hoffman Wood Trust Gold Medal.

THE BIENNALE, VENICE

Exhibition of works
by

JOHN CONSTABLE
MATTHEW SMITH
BARBARA HEPWORTH

organised by

THE BRITISH COUNCIL

1950

This Catalogue is not for sale

160 Catalogue cover of 25th Biennale at Venice

162 Venice — people moving

setting seemed to be vested with a new importance. But the most significant observation I made for my own work was that as soon as people, or groups of people, entered the Piazza they responded to the proportions of the architectural space. They walked differently, discovering their innate dignity. They grouped themselves in unconscious recognition of their importance in relation to each other as human beings. Apart from the Piazza, I noticed in Venice generally that there were particular movements of happiness springing from a mood among people which seemed to imbue them at once with greater swiftness and certainty of movement and gesture, and at the same time a greater relaxation.

THE SCULPTURES OF
BARBARA HEPWORTH

DAVID LEWIS

163 (above) Article by David Lewis
in *Eidos*. Illus. *Bicentric form* 1949–50

Sculptures of Barbara Hepworth

By DAVID LEWIS

164 Article by David Lewis
in *The Listener*, 27 July 1950.

165 (below) Catalogue of Lefevre
Gallery Exhibition, February 1950

No. 3   No. 7

No. 1   No. 2

6	Two figures	Elm, painted white	1947–48
7	Rhythmic form	Rosewood	1949
8	Eocene	Portland stone	1949
9	Two heads (Janus)	Mahogany	1949
10	Pendour	Wood with colour	1948
11	Perianth	Portland stone	1948
12	Dyad	Rosewood	1949
13	Pierced form	Alabaster	1949
14	Bimorphic theme	Mahogany	1949

STUDIES FOR SCULPTURE

Drawings and paintings in oil and pencil

(all executed in 1949 unless otherwise stated)

15 Seated girl (brown)
16 Seated girl (back view)
17 Two heads of Lisa (mauve)
18 Group seated on the ground
19 Two women (back view)
20 Group in shadow (back view)
21 Study of Lisa (front view)

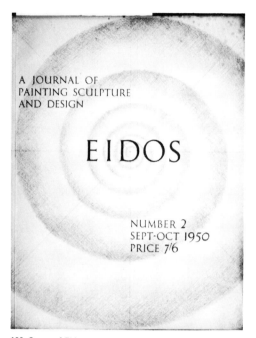

A JOURNAL OF
PAINTING SCULPTURE
AND DESIGN

EIDOS

NUMBER 2
SEPT·OCT 1950
PRICE 7/6

166 Cover of *Eidos*

167 Self-portrait in catalogue of
Wakefield Exhibition, July 1951

168 Article by J. P. Hodin in *Marmo 3*. Illus. *Group 1*

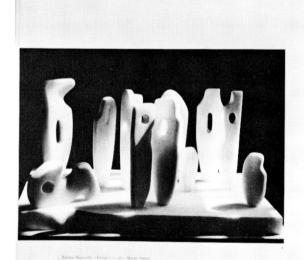

J. P. Hodin

Barbara Hepworth and the Mediterranean Spirit

Poets that lasting
marble seek
Must carve in Latin
or in Greek
Edmund Waller

We were sitting in the garden of Barbara Hepworth's « Trewyn » Studio in St. Ives. It was a late afternoon in the summer, the sky was blue, the bells of the nearby church sounded clear in the warm air. When the sound died down one could hear from afar the mighty roar of the waves which the flood threw against the sharp Cornish granite cliffs. The tops of the buildings and of the high trees here and there glowed up in the warm light of the setting sun. Under palm trees and flowering shrubs, between roses and gladioli some work of this outstanding English sculptor stood in the open. Nowhere in England has the spirit of the Mediterranean embodied itself so generously as here in this most Western strip of Cornwall, and nowhere in England is there an artist now at work who has expressed himself so perfectly in the medium of the classical style and its most beloved material — marble. It is true Barbara Hepworth has carved many a sculpture in tropical hardwood — blackwood, lignum vitae, ivorywood — in Spanish mahogany or in stone from near and far, she has even lately embarked on handling bronze but some of her most fascinating works are in marble and the artist herself, looking dreamily and relaxed at an unfinished sculpture after the day's hard work, said on that same afternoon when I remarked that we might be sitting somewhere in Greece or in Southern Italy, at Corinth or near Cuma where Aeneas landed on his flight from Troy — so unmistakably classical was the marble, the light and the sound of the South: « Yes, and how right to start with the marble, to continue with

light and to finish up with the sound of the whole, its music. Do you know that I love marble specially because of its radiance in the light, its hardness, precision and response to the sun? All this I learned to appreciate in Italy when I was a young student, and to have found this spot in Cornwall where nature corresponds so genuinely to my concept of style and my whole feeling has for years been a deep source of joy and satisfaction to me. To be quite correct; one of my earliest efforts, when a student in Chelsea, was to carve marble. The work got lost when I went abroad. But it was in Italy that I discovered truly the qualities of marble in its natural setting ».

And Barbara Hepworth, who was born in the coal-mining county of Yorkshire with its dark aspects of the industrial revolution and who, even as a young girl made a vow to bring beauty into that hell created by industrialism, to convey to her hard-working country-

Saint Ives

'ELECTRA' AT THE OLD VIC, LONDON

'THE UNKNOWN POLITICAL PRISONER'

RETROSPECTIVE AT THE WHITECHAPEL GALLERY

I VISIT GREECE

CREATED C.B.E. 1958

FIRST VISIT TO NEW YORK 1959

AWARDED THE 'GRAND PRIX' AT SAO PAULO BIENNIAL

169 Peggy Ashcroft as 'Electra', 1951

170 Playbill for *Electra*

171 *Apollo*, sculpture in steel rod for *Electra*

172 The set of *Electra*

BARBARA HEPWORTH

Carvings and Drawings

With an Introduction by Herbert Read

BARBARA HEPWORTH

CARVINGS AND DRAWINGS

LONDON: Lund Humphries & Co Ltd

173 *Barbara Hepworth,* Carvings and Drawings, book jacket

174 Title page

175 Frontispiece (*Curved forms* 1947)

curved forms   oil and pencil 22 × 15 p.m.3

1947

177 My son Paul, killed over
Thailand 13 February 1953

DEDICATION OF STATUE.

THE BISHOP:—Let us proceed to our Dedication in thankfulness in prayer, and in love.

Processional hymn E.H. 217, during which the Bishop blesses the incense and the procession is made to the Lady Chapel.

V. God, who at sundry times and in divers manners, spake in time past unto the fathers by the prophets.

R. Hath in these last days spoken unto us by his Son.

V. The angel Gabriel was sent from God.

R. To a virgin espoused to a man whose name was Joseph, of the house of David; and the virgin's name was Mary.

V. And the angel said unto her, Fear not, Mary: for thou hast found favour with God.

R. And behold thou shalt conceive in thy womb, and bring forth a son, and shalt call his name Jesus.

V. And the Word was made flesh.

R. And dwelt among us.

Prayer for the acceptance of the gift

O, Almighty Father, Lord of heaven and earth, who didst send thine only-begotten Son into the world that all might live through him: we beseech thee to accept this work at our hands, for the adornment of this thy House, and to consecrate our gift to thy glory for Jesus sake. Amen.

The Dedication

In the faith of Jesus Christ we dedicate this statue to the Glory of God and in memory of his servant Paul. In the Name of the Father, and of the Son, and of the Holy Ghost. Amen.

Collects

Almighty and everlasting God, who didst stoop to raise our fallen nature by the childbearing of Blessed Mary: Grant that we who have seen thy glory manifest in our manhood and thy love perfected in our weakness, may daily be renewed in thine image and conformed to the likeness of thy Son. Amen.

Remember in thy kingdom, O Lord Christ, those who counted not their lives dear unto themselves, but laid them down for their friends: Shed forth upon them the light of thy countenance, and grant that they may be numbered among the body of thy redeemed, going forth conquering and to conquer with thee; for evermore being Lord; who livest and reignest with the Father and the Holy Ghost, one God world without end. Amen.

THE SCULPTURE · MADONNA AND CHILD
(bianca del mare : height 31 inches)
is the work of BARBARA HEPWORTH, who carved it for St. Ives Parish Church in memory of her Son, Paul, who was killed on Active Service with the R.A.F. over Thailand, 13th February, 1953.

178 Service of Dedication of *Madonna and Child* in St Ives Parish Church

176 (opposite) *Madonna and Child* in St Ives Parish Church

179 Maquette for *The Unknown Political Prisoner*. Awarded a Second Prize in March 1953 (The Tate Gallery)

180 Cover of catalogue of Retrospective Exhibition at the Whitechapel Art Gallery, June 1954

182 View of the Retrospective Exhibition at the Whitechapel Art Gallery

181 *Monolith (Empyrean)*, (coll. Greater London Council)

The reason why people both move differently and stand differently in direct response to changed surroundings; the unconscious grouping of people when they are working together, producing a spatial movement that approximates to the structure of spirals in shells or rhythms in crystal structure; the meaning of the spaces between forms, or the shape of the displacement of forms in space, which in themselves have a most precise significance. All these responses spring from a factual and tactile approach to the object — whether it be the feeling of landscape that one feels beneath one's feet or the sensitivity of the hand in carving, or in surgery, or music, and they have an organic and perceptual purpose.

MISS BARBARA HEPWORTH

THE stars have not dealt me the worst they could do:
My pleasures are plenty, my troubles are two.
I'll never be cultured or decently fed
With holes in my stomach and string in my head.

B. A. Y. (after Housman)

381

183 *Punch* cartoon, 1954

184 Cover of *Architectural Review* May 1954 with *Concoid, Sphere and Hollow*, in front of Godrevy lighthouse

186 'Ritual Dance' constructions for 'The Midsummer Marriage.'

PORTRAIT GALLERY

SCULPTRESS

[Specially photographed for THE SUNDAY TIMES by DOUGLAS GL...]

Barbara Hepworth

NEXT Thursday evening will be important not only for Mr. Michael Tippett, whose opera "The Midsummer Marriage" will be given its first performance at Covent Garden, but also for Miss Barbara Hepworth, who has designed the scenery and costumes for the occasion.

Those who know the work of our leading woman sculptor will not be surprised to find that the temple which she has devised for "The Midsummer Marriage" has some resemblance to an intensified timber-yard, in which patches of pale colour have an effect out of all proportion to their simplicity. For Miss Hepworth is a carver, as much as a sculptor. Wood and its properties play a dominant part in her work; and so infectious is her understanding that a timber-merchant is known to have given her, almost on sight, two of his finest specimens.

* * *

AT first acquaintance it might be possible to mistake the huge-browed Miss Hepworth, with her firm, precise speech and neat habits of dress, for a professional intellectual. But she is, in fact, the mother of four children, including triplets—and a person who enjoys herself deeply and affectionately in the life that is around her. Miss Hepworth works out of doors, and for this reason has chosen to live in the warmest, most westerly part of England. By birth and upbringing she is a Yorkshire woman, reared in the West Riding, that true landscape," she has called it, "the source of man's energy."

The Sheraton among modern sculptors, strikingly and indeed exquisitely delicate, firm, nice in her handling of recalcitrant wood or stone, Miss Hepworth sees for rather fewer work from the point of view of a dedicated professional who can deal as effectively with complexities of Himalayan rosewood as with small aggravations of nursery and kitchen. Ives is her home, but both in Whitechapel, her big retrospective exhibition last year a genuine furore, and in the companionable tumult of the Royal Opera House she is a well liked and well-respected visitor.

I first got to know Michael Tippett well in 1952 when we were all working on the idea of the St. Ives Festival of Music which took place in June 1953. It was in 1954 that he approached me about the sets for The Midsummer Marriage. We discussed it, sitting in my garden; and for the next months I had the opportunity of seeing him at work and of appreciating more and more his remarkable powers of disciplined and yet inspired co-operation. I think The Midsummer Marriage asked, in both its allegorical meaning and its symbolism, for a new discipline; also for a new tradition, perhaps related to the formality of Greek theatre or of the Mystery Plays. This demand should, I felt, be developed and fulfilled. On traditional lines, the unwieldy passion of the chorus could be an asset. But in unconventional presentations, musically, the chorus was needed only as voice and, both musically and in mass, should be as disciplined as part of an orchestra and not produced dramatically.

The English find a romantic idea easier to accept; but I still have an absolute faith in the classical development even in opera (that most difficult of all the arts), and I believe that just round the corner, as Michael Tippett saw, the composer can find a new form which will in the future be full of meaning for our society.

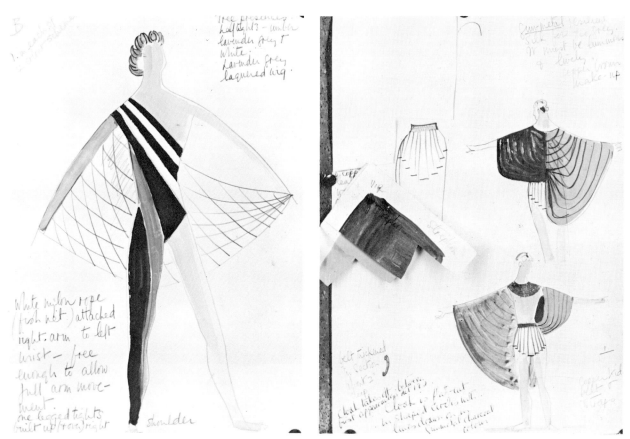

187 & 188 Designs for costumes for 'The Midsummer Marriage' at the Royal Opera House, Covent Garden, January 1955.

189 The Corps de Ballet in 'Ritual Dance'

In Greece the inspiration was fantastic. I ran up the hills like a hare, with my notebook, to get there first and have the total impact of solitude. I made many drawings for new sculptures called 'Delphi', 'Delos', 'Mycenae', Epidauros' and 'Santorin'. These forms were my experience there. After my solitude I waited for the 199 people I had left behind, and watched their movements and responses on entering the architecture in the superb location of mountain, hill and plain. This was very anti-social, I admit; but I had waited thirty years to get to Greece.

These notes were written around the edges of my sketch-book:

COLOURS *Indigo sea, which when light reflects from cliffs, becomes pure cerulean. Thin indian red and pink hills – monastral purple mountains at sunset, which intensifies the greens to the wildest vitality.*

The Acropolis – the spaces between the columns – the depth of flutings to touch – the breadth, weight and volume – the magnificence of a single marble, bole up-ended. The passionate warm colour of the marble and all-pervading philosophic proportion and space.

NAUPLION *– a serene and lovely port.*

MYCENAE *– a rhythmic movement of mountains.*

The Royal Tombs – a vast ellipse (pit) of stones on stones.

Majestic landscape, hills purple and pink, blue and some deep red – the lower margin of hills rhythmic with olives; the upper hills rhythmic with folds from left to right.

The nearest hill, a high one (many such) but this is high and grand. Studded with stones and green mounds of low growing verdure.

The site itself is of great beauty and majesty – a high throne thrust from the higher hills and facing Argos Plains – the vista so great in depth and breadth that the gods command all.

The view back through the Lion's Gate – the grandeur of the Royal Tomb looking towards the mountains with Argos on the left – the Treasury of Atreus and its noble proportion – the beehive within – the great curved supporting stone and the use of the triangle.

Only sign of growth, tobacco and olives – the corn gathered in April.

All the landscape forms of Greece tend to elevate the human figure – column and Core are inevitable.

DELOS *Ascended Kynthes alone, the cave of Apollo – half way magnificent and majestic. A pool with fine fig trees nearby full of giant (sacred?) toads – leaping and barking. Also green frogs.*

Went on alone up the last steep ascent, but the wind was angry – ferocious. I fell, my hair was nearly whisked off my head – my clothes nearly torn off me. I bowed to the will of the gods and descended.

Saw a magnificent Koros – tall, fierce and passionate, bigger than life-size – in the museum. A heavenly work – the back and buttocks in relation to the hip and waist – an inspiration. I thought the fragment of leg and calf (attached below the knee) was falsely attributed . . .

BARBARA HEPWORTH

Carvings and Drawings

1937–1954

WALKER ART CENTER
April 15–May 29, 1955

THE UNIVERSITY OF NEBRASKA ART GALLERIES
June 15–August 15, 1955

SAN FRANCISCO MUSEUM OF ART
September 1–October 16, 1955

THE ALBRIGHT ART GALLERY
November 9–December 15, 1955

THE ART GALLERY OF TORONTO
January 1–February 15, 1956

THE MONTREAL MUSEUM OF FINE ARTS
March 1–March 31, 1956

THE BALTIMORE MUSEUM OF ART
April 15–June 30, 1956

This exhibition is arranged through the courtesy of the
MARTHA JACKSON GALLERY   22 East 66 Street, New York

191 Retrospective Travelling Exhibition opening
at Martha Jackson Gallery, New York

192 In the workshop with *Corinthos*

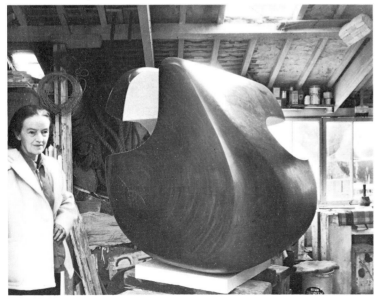

193 *Pastorale,* marble, placed in the
Rijksmuseum Kröller-Müller, Otterlo, Holland

This was a most exciting period. A friend
had asked for samples of Nigerian wood to
be sent to me. Suddenly I got a note from the
docks to say that 17 tons of wood had arrived
at Tilbury Docks and would I please collect.

Mercifully a strike occurred (mercifully
for me!) and it gave me time to try to arrange
transport.

The difficulties were immense. The smallest piece weighed $\frac{3}{4}$ of a ton. The largest
weighed 2 tons. It became a drama in St. Ives.
Each piece of wood had a giant fork driven
into it, and a huge metal ring (no doubt to
enable elephants or cranes to lift each piece),
but in the cobbled streets of St. Ives we had
to man-handle each piece. This was the drama.
The logs were the biggest and finest I had
ever seen — most beautiful, hard, lovely warm
timber. Out of these 'samples' I carved
'Corinthos', 'Delphi', 'Phira', 'Epidauros'
and 'Delos'. I was never happier.

72

194 In my garden

195 Catalogue cover of Exhibition at Gimpel Fils Gallery

196 Marble and tools in the stoneyard, Trewyn Studio

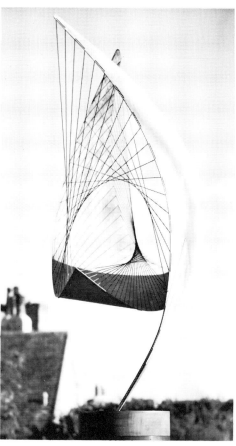

197 *Theme on Electronics,* 47 in. Commissioned for Mullard House, London

198 Pages 98 and 99 of *La sculpture de ce siècle by* Michel Seuphor

Barbara Hepworth, Figure, 1956

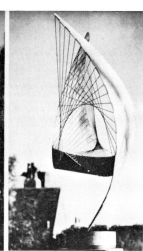

Barbara Hepworth, Orphee, 1956

s'oriente vers une conception plus sociale et nettement figurative (*Groupe de famille*, 1945-1949; le *Fauteuil à bascule*, 1950; *Figure appuyée*, 1951; *Femme et enfant dans un fauteuil latte*, 1952), accusant parfois des réminiscences grecques, d'ailleurs admirablement assimilées et récrites (*Figure drapée, couchée; Guerrier avec bouclier; Femme assise sur un banc*, tous de 1953). En même temps il continue les figures abstraites ou presque abstraites (relief mural à Rotterdam, 1955; *Figure debout*, 1950; *Trois figures debout*, 1953), ou même abstraites tout à fait (cloison pour le Time-life Building, a

Barbara Hepworth, Deux menhirs, 1955

99

for catalogue Holland Park Sculpture Exhibition

Barbara Hepworth

" Curved form (Trevalgan) "

This "Curved form" was conceived standing on the hill called Trevalgan between St. Ives and Zennor where the land of Cornwall ends and the cliffs divide as they touch the sea facing west.
At this point, facing the setting sun across the Atlantic, where sky and sea blend with hills and rocks, the forms seem to enfold the watcher and lift him towards the sky.

Dec 1956   Barbara Hepworth

199 Statement on *Curved form (Trevalgan)* : Holland Park Sculpture Exhibition, 1957

201 Carving *Fugue II,* Irish marble

200 My cat Nicholas

I had by this time become bewitched by the Atlantic beach. The form I call Porthmeor is the ebb and flow of the Atlantic.

Here I pay tribute to Bernard Leach and Janet Leach who gave so much to the ever increasing contact of east and west. Patrick Heron and Brian Wynter and their families were living at Zennor. Terry Frost, Denis Mitchell and many, many others had their studios in the town. So had Priaulx Rainier who, in the early fifties, had done so much with Michael Tippett to create the St. Ives Festival.

We all felt the fast growing understanding of art round the world and the international language which had been created — we may have lived at Lands End but we were in close contact with the whole world.

Looking out from our studios on the Atlantic beach we became more deeply rooted in Europe; but straining at the same time to fly like a bird over 3,000 miles of water towards America and the East to unite our philosophy, religion and aesthetic language.

202 Created C.B.E. in New Year Honours List, 1958

203 Book jacket of *Hepworth* by A. M. Hammacher: *Curved form (Delphi)*

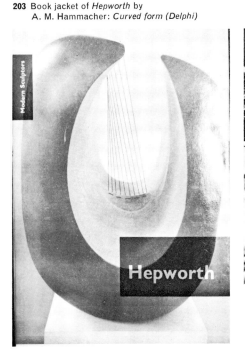

204 Frontispiece and title page of *Hepworth* (in Modern Sculptors Series)

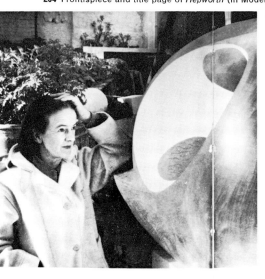

76

205 *Sea form (Porthmeor),* bronze, 46 in. (at Middelheimpark, Antwerp)

206 The hands of Bernard Leach

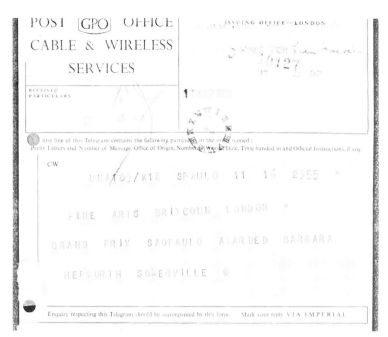

207 The telegram that informed me of the Grand Prix Award at Sao Paulo Biennial

208 Cutting from the *Scotsman*

209 Cover of catalogue of Vth Sao Paulo Biennial, September 1959

TOP AWARD FOR U.K. SCULPTOR

Barbara Hepworth's Brazil triumph

The British sculptor Barbara Hepworth has won the major award at the International Bienniel Exhibition of Modern Art which opens at Sao Paulo (Brazil), this week-end. It is worth about £1600. This is the first time a British artist has won the prize.

In 1953, Henry Moore won the prize for the best foreign sculptor, and in 1957 Ben Nicholson won that for the best foreign painter.

The award won by Miss Hepworth, known as the "Prize of the Sao Paulo Prefecture," is open to all artists in whatever medium they work.

Miss Hepworth, who was notified by telegram from Brazil, said she had sent representative work done over the past 20 years. It included 20 sculptures, wood carvings, works in stone, marble carvings and bronzes. She also submitted 17 drawings of her sculptures.

When I got the telegram from Sao Paulo I wandered about the garden, not believing it. All thanks are due to Mrs Lilian Somerville who went out to Sao Paulo and got these large works off the floor and onto their feet.

I felt ill and unable to travel. My doctor, when called, would always ask me 'is this a pre-exhibition or a post-exhibition illness?'. I literally thrive on quiet hard work at home; but get an emotional panic over exhibitions.

Exhibition organized by the British Council
Exposición organizada por el British Council

BARBARA HEPWORTH

210 Title page and list of subsequent exhibitions 1959-60 in Vth Sao Paulo Biennial catalogue

V Bienal do Museu de Arte Moderna Sao Paulo 1959
Comisión National de Bellas Artes, Montevideo 1960
Museo Nacional de Bellas Artes, Buenos Aires 1960
Instituto de Arte Moderno, Santiago 1960
Museo de Bellas Artes, Caracas 1960

a new decade

MY GRANDCHILDREN

FRIENDSHIP WITH DAG HAMMARSKJOLD

'SINGLE FORM' COMMISSIONED FOR U.N.

MAJOR RETROSPECTIVE AT THE TATE GALLERY

THE FREEDOM OF ST. IVES

HEPWORTH

GALERIE CHALETTE   1100 MADISON AVE.   NEW YORK

211 Title page of Galerie Chalette Exhibition catalogue

212 My hands

213 First page of introduction by Herbert Read for
the catalogue of Galerie Chalette Exhibition 1959

*My left hand is my thinking hand. The right
is only a motor hand. This holds the hammer.
The left hand, the thinking hand, must be
relaxed, sensitive. The rhythms of thought
pass through the fingers and grip of this hand
into the stone.*

   *It is also a listening hand. It listens for
basic weaknesses of flaws in the stone; for
the possibility or imminence of fractures.*

A LETTER OF INTRODUCTION

By Sir Herbert Read

My dear Barbara:

When I heard that Dr. Lejwa wanted me to write an introduction to this
catalogue, my first instinct was to refuse—just because I have written so
many such introductions, and the convention becomes a little stale. Espe-
cially in your case, I felt I could not once again offer my inadequate words
as a buffer between the uninitiated visitor to the exhibition and the works
themselves, in all their plastic innocence. I began a letter to you to make
my excuses, and in writing the letter I found I had something to say, and
that I was saying it in an unconventional way. And so the letter became this
introduction.

It is more than a quarter of a century since you found me a neighbouring
studio in Hampstead, where a group that included Henry Moore, Ben Nicholson and Paul Nash, worked in close proximity until dispersed by the out-
break of war. The beginning of that experience is recorded in UNIT ONE, the
book we published together in 1934. When I turn the pages of this book

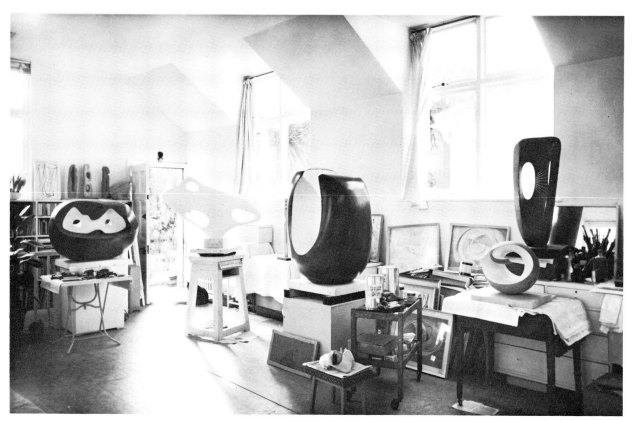

214 Trewyn Studio, January 1959

I became more and more pre-occupied with the inside and outside of forms as I had been in the late 1930's, but on a bigger scale. I wanted to make forms to stand on hillsides and through which to look to the sea. Forms to lie down in, or forms to climb through. I would go out at night to see the effect of moonlight and then wait for the rising sun and make notes as to what happened then.

215 *Curved form with inner form (Anima)*, bronze, 27¾ in.

We are so placed here, geographically, that both sun and moon rise and set over the water with a great radiance and this fact sets up a remarkable tension in my everyday life. I am not scientifically minded; but the forces between the everchanging position of the sun and moon, and the effects upon sea and tide, and cloud and wind, which change the depth of shadow on forms have governed my life for a long time.

I began to get more and more turn-tables and to try to assess my own changing movements in relation to the sun.

Piercings through forms became dominant. Could I climb through and in what direction? Could I rest, lie or stand within the forms? Could I, at one and the same time, be the outside as well as the form within?

Coming back from America after one of my visits, I became so unutterably bored by the false surroundings in the aircraft, the colour T.V., cigar smoke and champagne that I begged permission to go into the cockpit and make a drawing of the sunrise. Permission was granted and it was one of the great experiences of my life.

The pilot said, quite frankly, that he thought I was a bit silly and that he, personally, was tired of sun-rises. But quite apart from the super-natural colours and shapes, and the sense of real flying, I think I was even more deeply impressed by the utter ease of movement by pilot and co-pilot and navigator in such incredibly restricted space.

To go on seemed sensible. To descend a very hard discipline. I would like to be an astronaut and go round the moon, and maybe remain in orbit for ever. But I would not like to land in case the light of the moon went out forever and all poetry die and deeper anguish descend on this anguished earth. But my son Paul once told me that there was a new aesthetic in flying and space and maybe these many brave men will guide us.

216 With *Figure (Archaean)* in the garden

217 Party to celebrate casting of *Meridian* at Susse Frères Foundry, Paris

218 *Meridian*, 1958-9, Bronze, 15 ft
(commissioned for State House, London)

219 *Meridian* in situ (unveiled 17 March 1960)

When, in July 1960, Birmingham University conferred upon me an Honorary Degree, I was deeply moved. The whole ceremony was inspiring.
For so many years I had been shut away in the kitchen or nursery, or in my studio, covered with dust & chippings. The colourful procedures of the ceremony, & the co-ordination of University life, allowed me, for a brief moment, to share in those intentions & movements of group life which have always fascinated me; and of which I have written in the past in relation to Venice & the operating theatre.
The Honour, of course, delighted me.

220 Hon. D. Litt., Birmingham University

It was a sad day when these cottages opposite my house were demolished. No repairs had been done, no amenities laid on, and the value of the land came before all else.

In 1954 the St. Ives Trust was formed, representing a number of local societies who wished to preserve the character of the old town, and to develop it in the spirit of our ancestors, who had such an innate understanding of the use of indigenous material, and a sense of the shape of the land and protection it gave from storms. In 1967 the Trust became the Friends of St. Ives, with individual membership.

Naturally, after 150 years or more, roofs sink and timbers rot. But with the help of many devoted people, old fish cellars and other ancient structures have been saved and rebuilt to make a reconstitution of all that

BARBARA HEPWORTH

221 Front and back covers of the catalogue of my Exhibition at Galerie Charles Lienhard, Zurich, October 1960

222 *Totem*, white marble, 54 in. (coll. Peter Stuyvesant Foundation)

223 Outside my workshop door in Ayr Lane

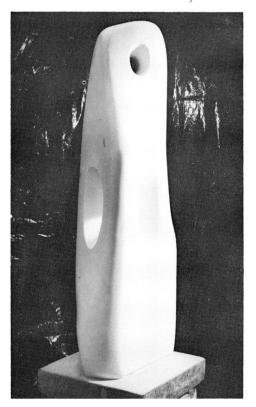

people so much love in this small town. After some 120 years, my own studio is getting very shaky indeed. It is on a famous corner of old St. Ives, and, though repairs are essential, I want above all to keep its character and preserve its quality.

224 Simon's wife Silvie and daughter Minka

225 Simon in St. Ives

226 Simon's children Tuula and Minka

Grandchildren are the greatest delight and I think everyone would agree with me. It is for the grandparents one of the happiest relationships life can offer.

Gone are the sleepless nights wondering what to do for the best for the children: and here are all these eager spirits and vital young bodies growing like plants under my eyes, each with a most decisive personality.

I think they regard a grandparent as a piece of known and loved furniture. Either we are a bit of rock on the beach, or a favourite tree in the garden — but always an accepted bit of the landscape. They laugh at me and tease me; they bring presents of drawings

227 Sarah and Alan Bowness in my garden

228 Sarah with my first grandson Paul

229 The carving yard at Trewyn Studio
230 Sarah's children Paul and Sophie

and paintings, pebbles and shells; always with a penetrating glance and a humorous smile and a gentle touch. They give me the great gift of being carefree and happy.

What happens when one has great-grandchildren I do not know. I remember my own very gay great-grandmother with affection; but these days, maybe, it might be different. Perhaps a cooler and more disciplined approach to natural ties? . . .

I love my blocks of marble, always piling up in the yard like a flock of sheep.

BARBARA HEPWORTH

231 Frontispiece and title page of *Barbara Hepworth, Life and Work* by J. P. Hodin (1961)

233 Rachel's son Jeremy

232 Cover of *Barbara Hepworth, Life and Work :* Illus. *Serene Head (Thea),* 1959

234 Rachel's daughter Allison

235 Julia, third child of Rachel and Michael Kidd

BARBARA HEPWORTH

236 (above) *Hollow form (Churinga III),* lignum vitae, 30 in. (coll. Dag Hammarskjöld Museum, Backakra, Sweden)

237 *Single form (September)* 1961, walnut, 33 in.

238 Photograph of Dag Hammarskjöld on cover of *United Nations News* July-Sept. 1960

240 *Single form (memorial)* Bronze, 10 ft 3 in. (Coll. Greater London Council: in Battersea Park)

239 Cover of Memorial Service to Dag Hammarskjöld at Westminster Abbey, October 1961

WESTMINSTER ABBEY

DAG HAMMARSKJOLD
Secretary General of the United Nations
1953 — 1961

died
18 SEPTEMBER 1961

*How blest are the peace-
makers; God shall call
them his sons*

MEMORIAL SERVICE
23 OCTOBER 1961
at 12 noon

241 The new studio

242 *Reclining form (Rosewall)* in Trewyn Studio garden prior to its siting at Chetwynd House, Chesterfield

243 My new studio in March 1961

Obtaining this new studio and workshop was a strange experience. For many years it had been a Palais de Danse, with the thump of drums keeping me awake.

Suddenly it closed and quiet prevailed. Then, one night, I awakened to the fact that here on my doorstep was a perfect studio and workshop. I could barely wait till dawn and, remembering Marcus Brumwell's advice over Trewyn, I rang up the owner and bought it.

Strangely, it has become the most quiet workshop. I worked happily from the moment .I took over; and here my friend of two decades, and for long my helper and secretary Margaret Moir, takes charge. Suddenly the noise has abated and thanks to her peace prevails and works come and go.

244 Marcus Brumwell
245 Rene Brumwell

246 Drawing the landscape on Rosewall, St Ives (from B.B.C. Television film 'Barbara Hepworth' produced by John Read)

247 *Reclining form (Rosewall)* at Chetwynd House, Chesterfield

248 Hon. D. Litt., University of Leeds

Leeds.

In 1961, the University of Leeds conferred upon me an Hon. D. Litt. & I travelled north to my native land the first time for many years. The honour meant very much to me, &, in addition, the warmth of welcome & the gentle intonation of the West Riding. Again the colourful ceremony really moved me; but, alas, the bitter cold east wind drove me back to Cornwall & I realised how much sun, warmth & light mean to my work.

Although my Yorkshire background means so very much to me, &, indeed disciplined me to the life of form & sculpture, I realised that it was only by breaking away from the rigours & darkness of the north that I could really give praise to the Yorkshire background which raised me & trained me

249 Simon with *Winged figure* (detail)

250 *Turning form* (blue on a pink ground). Oil and pencil, 19⅝ x 12⅛ in.

251 252 & 254 *Winged figure* in transit through St Ives, 1962

253 *Winged figure,* 19 ft high (commissioned by John Lewis Partnership Ltd), on John Lewis Building, Oxford Street, London

254

BARBARA HEPWORTH

*an exhibition of sculpture
from 1952-1962
Whitechapel Art Gallery*

255 Title page and frontispiece of catalogue of Retrospective Exhibition 1952-62, Whitechapel Art Gallery: Illus. *Figure (Archaean)*

256 *Pierced form,* Pentelicon white marble, 50 in.

258 Book jacket (1963)

257 *Square form with circles.* Bronze, 8 ft 6 in. at the Israel Museum Jerusalem

May 27, 1963

AWARD

Barbara Hepworth

This is to certify that your work

"*Archaean*" exhibited at the
7th International Art Exhibition of Japan
sponsored by the Mainichi Newspapers and the
Japan International Art Promotion Association,

was awarded the

Foreign Minister Award

Tsunetaka Ueda
President, The Mainichi
Newspapers
Chairman, The Japan Int'l
Art Promotion Association

259 'Foreign Minister's Award' given to me at
the 7th International Art Exhibition, Tokyo

賞 状

バーバラ、ヘプワース殿

毎日新聞社日本国際美術振興会
主催第七回日本国際美術展に
出品されたあなたの作品「古代人」
は選考の結果外務大臣賞に推
されました ここにこの賞を贈り
栄誉をたたえます

一九六三年五月

毎日新聞社社長

日本国際美術振興会理事長

上田常隆

260 Scroll of 'Foreign Minister's Award'

261 With *Vertical form*, stone, in the carving yard at Trewyn Studio

*All landscape needs a figure — and when a
sculptor is the spectator he is aware that every
landscape evokes a special image. In creating
this image the artist tries to find a synthesis of
his human experience and the quality of the
land-scape. The forms and piercings, the
weight and poise of the concrete image also
become evocative — a fusion of experience and
myth.*

*Working in the abstract way seems to
release one's personality and sharpen the
perceptions so that in the observation of
humanity or landscape it is the wholeness of
inner intention which moves one so profoundly.
The components fall into place and one is no
longer aware of the detail except as the
necessary significance of wholeness and unity
. . . a rhythm of form which has its roots in
earth but reaches outwards towards the unknown experiences of the future. The thought
underlying this form is, for me, the delicate
balance the spirit of man maintains between
his knowledge and the laws of the universe.*

262 Working on the first stage of *Single form*

Before Dag Hammarskjöld's death we had discussed together the kind of form he had envisaged to go in front of the Secretariat. When I heard of his death, and in order to assuage my grief, I immediately made a large new version of Single Form just for myself. It was 10 ft. 6 in. high.

Later, when the Secretary General heard of this, he asked me if I would go to New York and discuss the project as Dag Hammarskjöld had envisaged it.

Between us all we arrived at the right scale and position; and I met with the utmost kindness and help. Then for some months I had to work to the scale of 21 feet and bring into my mind everything my father had taught me about stress and strain and gravity and windforce. Finally, all the many parts were got out of St. Ives safely, and when assembled in a big London studio they stood up in perfect balance. This was a magic moment. Finally the whole work was complete, and went to New York.

Memorial *Single form* to Dag Hammarskjöld at the United Nations Secretariat. Commissioned by United Nations. Ht 21 ft

263 A discussion with Sebastian Halliday in my studio

264 Plaster of *Single form*

265 The final stage of *Single form,* bronze, at The Morris Singer Foundry in April, 1964

ADDRESS AT THE UNVEILING OF 'SINGLE FORM' IN NEW YORK, 11 JUNE 1964

It is very difficult for me to speak, because I can only communicate through my sculpture but I would like to offer these few words.

Dag Hammarskjöld spoke to me often about the evolution of the 'Single Form' in relation to compassion, and to courage and to our creativity. When I heard of his death, and sharing my grief with countless thousands of people, my only thought was to carry out his wishes.

Dag Hammarskjöld had a pure and exact perception of aesthetic principles, as exact as it was over ethical and moral principles. I believe they were, to him, one and the same thing, and he asked of each of us the best we could give.

The United Nations is our conscience. If it succeeds it is our success. If it fails it is our failure. Throughout my work on the 'Single Form' I have kept in mind Dag Hammarskjöld's ideas of human and aesthetic ideology and I have tried to perfect a symbol that would reflect the nobility of his life, and at the same time give us a motive and symbol of both continuity and solidarity for the future.

266 Delivering a short address at the unveiling of *Single form*

268 *Single form*

267 With U Thant, Secretary General, before the unveiling of *Single form*

PROGRAMME
OF THE UNVEILING
OF

SINGLE FORM
by BARBARA HEPWORTH
Gift of JACOB BLAUSTEIN
after a wish of
DAG HAMMARSKJOLD

11 June 1964
UNITED NATIONS
NEW YORK

Dag Hammarskjold had often privately expressed the wish that the circle in front of the Secretariat building at the United Nations would one day be adorned with an appropriate sculpture. He had also indicated his view that such a work of art might be most suitably executed by his friend, Miss Barbara Hepworth, of England whose work is greatly admired. This wish has now been fulfilled in memory of the late Secretary-General. It has been made possible by the interest and generosity of Jacob Blaustein of Baltimore, a former United States delegate to the United Nations and a personal friend of Mr. Hammarskjold. The sculpture is a free-form abstraction, entitled Single Form. It stands twenty-one feet high on a granite plinth and has been cast in bronze in the foundry of the Morris Singer Company, London, England.

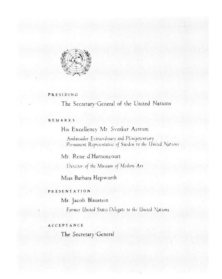

PRESIDING
The Secretary-General of the United Nations

REMARKS
His Excellency Mr. Sverker Astrom
Ambassador Extraordinary and Plenipotentiary
Permanent Representative of Sweden to the United Nations

Mr. Rene d'Harnoncourt
Director of the Museum of Modern Art

Miss Barbara Hepworth

PRESENTATION
Mr. Jacob Blaustein
Former United States Delegate to the United Nations

ACCEPTANCE
The Secretary-General

269 Programme of the unveiling of *Single form* at United Nations, 11 June 1964; **(270)** Introduction: **(271)** List of speakers

272 Aerial view of the ceremony

273 *Single form* in situ, New York

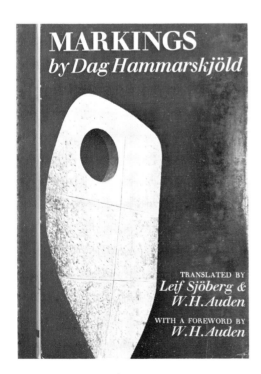

274 Book jacket *Markings* by Dag Hammarskjöld

In the lives of most men there is some form of tension between the attraction of the world outside and their yearning for home. Dag Hammarskjold, with his searching mind, felt more than most men the attraction of journeying along new roads and he travelled far and wide in the world. But always he carried in his heart the image of his Swedish homeland. As the years went by in New York his thoughts began to linger more and more on his return to Sweden and the home he intended to make for himself there.

In this connection the enclosed square of this Skane farm came to appear as ideal at an early stage. In his account of Skepparps-garden at Havang Dag Hammarskjold himself described the tranquil space formed by the courtyard plan of this type of house.

The Skane courtyard shuts out the wind and the eyes of unauthorised persons but retains the sun's warmth for enjoyment on the stone step or on a bench along the hollyhock-covered wall of the house. To the man who, after long years of wandering, is making his way home to rest and to concentrate on his own ground, such a dwelling must have seemed attractive.

275 Visit to the Dag Hammarskjöld Museum at Backakra, Sweden

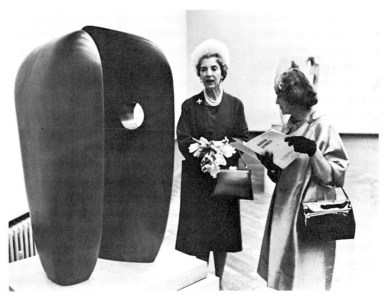

276 Opening of the Retrospective British Council Exhibition at Copenhagen, in the presence of H.M. Queen Ingrid of Denmark

277 Catalogue cover of the Retrospective British Council Exhibition in Stockholm

5

BARBARA HEPWORTH
Moderna Museet
Stockholm 1964

278 In my studio, May 1964

279 Completion of *Marble with colour (Crete),* white marble,
54½ in., now in Museum Boymans van-Bueningen, Rotterdam, Holland

An exhibition of drawings.
paintings and sculpture

Marlborough Fine Art Limited
39 Old Bond Street
London W1
Telephone: Mayfair 5161

and

Marlborough New London Gallery
17.18 Old Bond Street
London W1
Telephone: Mayfair 5161

Exhibition open
12 March-15 April 1965
Daily 10 am-5 pm
Saturdays 10 am-12 pm

Art in Britain 1930-40 centred around Axis Circle Unit One

Eileen Agar
John Armstrong
Winifred Dacre
Merlyn Evans
Naum Gabo
Ashley Havinden
Barbara Hepworth
Tristram Hillier
Charles Howard
Arthur Jackson
Roy de Maistre
Piet Mondrian
Henry Moore
Alastair Morton
Paul Nash
Ben Nicholson
John Piper
Victor Reinganum
Ceri Richards
Cecil Stephenson
John Tunnard
Edward Wadsworth

280 'Art in Britain 1930-40' Exhibition

281 Certificate of the Granting of the Dignity of an Ordinary Dame Commander of the Civil Division of the Order of the British Empire, 12 June 1965

282 Catalogue cover of the Retrospective Exhibition at Basel, September/October 1965

. . . Ever since 1953 my predecessor had tried to visualise such a blending of perceptions by creating a garden around the museum landscaped for sculpture. Finally in 1961 this garden was opened and to the nucleus of the collection of sculptures, which since the summer of that year has been exhibited in a natural setting, belong two of Barbara Hepworth's bronzes: "Archaic Form" 1958 and "Anima" 1959 . . .'

QUOTED FROM DR R OXENAAR (TATE GALLERY CATALOGUE)

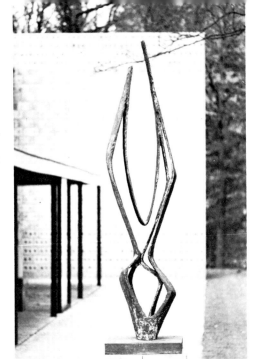

285 With Professor A. M. Hammacher, Dr Paul Hodin
and Dr Renilde Hammacher at
the opening of the Retrospective Exhibition at the
Rijksmuseum Kröller-Müller on the occasion
of the opening of the new Rietveld Pavilion

283 (left) *Cantate Domino,* Bronze, 80 in.,
at the Rijksmuseum Kröller-Müller

284 (below) *Squares with two circles,* bronze, 10 ft 4 in.
(Rijksmuseum Kröller-Müller, Otterlo)

286 *Sea form (Atlantic).* Bronze, 78 in.

287 Catalogue cover of exhibition at the Marlborough-Gerson Gallery, New York, April-May 196▊

288 Introduction to my catalogue by Herbert Read; The Marlborough-Gerson Gallery, New York

Barbara Hepworth
by Herbert Read

Dame Barbara Hepworth has written so revealingly about the art of sculpture that little is left for the critic to say except to point out how perfectly she has realized her own ideals. In so far as these ideals have been technical she has shown her perfect mastery of the art of carving and more recently has become proficient in the process of bronze-casting.

The particular revelation of recent years — and this exhibition is devoted to the work of recent years — is the manner in which she has related the process of casting to 'the sculptural idea'. Fourteen years ago, in her preface to *Carvings and Drawings*, the volume which reviewed her work up to that date, she declared that 'carving to me is a necessary approach — one facet of the whole idea which will remain valid for all time. It is, in fact, a biological necessity as it is concerned with aspects of living of which we cannot afford to be deprived'. In the autobiographical notes on her career that followed in the volume she made quite clear what she meant by this somewhat mystical doctrine. Carving is an extension of the telluric forces that mould the landscape. The sculptor is seen as a sensitive figure in that landscape responding as she carves to the ever-changing pattern of the forms around her. She describes the process with a lyrical passion no poet could rival:

'The sea, a flat diminishing plane, held within itself the capacity to radiate an infinitude of blues, greys, greens, and even pinks of strange hues: the lighthouse and its strange rocky island was an eye: the Island of St Ives an arm, a hand, a face. The rock formation of the great bay had a withinness of form which led my imagination straight to the country of West Penwith behind me although the visual thrust was straight out to sea. The incoming and receding tides made strange and wonderful calligraphy on the pale granite sand which sparkled with felspar and mica. The rich mineral deposits of Cornwall were apparent on the very surface of things; quartz, amethyst, and topaz; tin and copper below in the old mine shafts; and geology and pre-history — a thousand facts induced a thousand fantasies of form and purpose, structure and life, which had gone into the making of what I saw and what I was.'

It will be seen that the morphology described is essentially structural; and the sculpture that reflects it is also structural. In passing from carving to bronze-casting Barbara Hepworth has not abandoned this structural consistency. Her forms remain essentially crystalline and calligraphic. At one time my first reaction was to question this replication of a form conceived in terms of organic materials such as wood and marble in a man-made alloy of copper and tin; and the fact that bronze flows into a prepared mould seemed to contradict the sculptural idea in so far as it is an affirmation of 'some ancient stability'. But I have now come to realize that what I previously discerned as the artist's fundamental purpose, 'to infuse the formal perfection of geometry with the vital grace of nature', is as fully realized in bronze as in carved wood or stone, and is more durable in this material. Durability, oddly enough, is an aesthetic virtue.

Nevertheless, for Barbara Hepworth carving remains the primary activity, and she has never so completely demonstrated her mastery of this art as in the work of the last ten years. Whether we consider the *Menhirs 1964* which are in teak, or the *Pierced Monolith with colour* (1965) which is in Roman stone, or the several forms in slate (1965), the craftsmanship is of a perfection which only Brancusi among modern sculptors has previously attained, and as examples of geometry infused with the vital grace of nature, these pieces seem to me to excel any of the artist's own earlier works.

Barbara Hepworth has been greatly honoured in her own country and her fame is now world-wide. At this stage in an artist's career it is fatally easy to relax, to accept the plaudits of the public as a belated but sufficient reward for a life-time of struggle and neglect. It is characteristic of Barbara Hepworth (as it is of the artists who have been most closely associated with her, Ben Nicholson and Henry Moore) that success has brought with it no diminution of energy or of invention: these recent works are not only a fulfilment of ideals that have been firmly maintained throughout a career of nearly forty years; they are also at the same time evidence of an unending search for some final truth or beauty. The more the forms change, the more clearly Form itself, as the symbol of universal order or superhuman perfection, stands revealed.

Sculptures illustrated on front and back covers, frontispiece and small text illustrations were photographed in the garden of Dame Barbara's Trewyn studio at St Ives, Cornwall, 1965.

UNIVERSITY OF EXETER

At a Congregation held in the
University on   *May 10, 1966*   the
Degree of DOCTOR OF LETTERS
honoris causa was conferred upon
Barbara Hepworth

Mary Cadbury   , *Chancellor*

Ivan G. Smith   *Academic Registrar*

289 Honorary Degree – Hon. D. Litt. – conferred
by Exeter University, 10 May 1966

290 At Exeter University on the occasion of the conferment

291 *River form,* American walnut, 74 in.

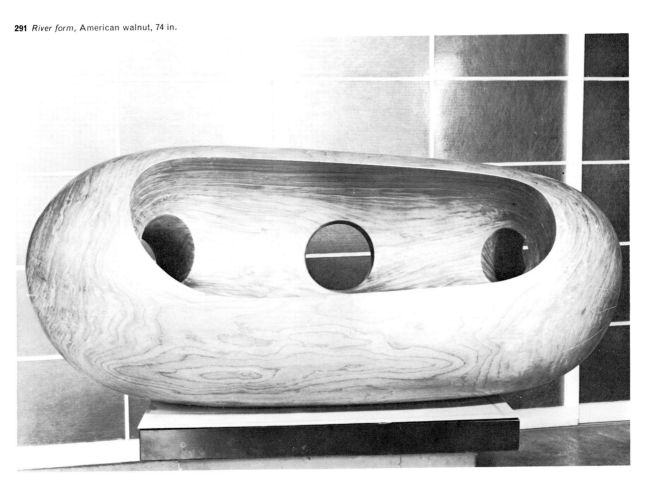

293 *Construction (Crucifixion)* Bronze with colour, 12ft, photographed in St Ives Parish Churchyard

295 (below) With Professor A. M. Hammacher and Miss
Pat Loman of Thames & Hudson in my garden

296 (below right) Discussing a new book to be written by Professor
Hammacher, with the author and Mrs A. M. Hammacher

294 Mimi

298 My kitten Tobey

299 Trewyn Studio

The sculptor must search with passionate intensity for the underlying principle of the organisation of mass and tension — the meaning of gesture and the structure of rhythm.

In my search for these values I like to work both realistically and abstractly. In my drawing and painting I turn from one to the other as a necessity or impulse and not because of a preconceived design of action. When drawing what I see I am usually most conscious of the underlying principle of abstract form in human beings and their relationship one to the other. In making my abstract drawings I am most often aware of those human values which dominate the structure and meaning of abstract forms.

Sculpture is the fusion of these two attitudes and I like to be free as to the degree of abstraction and realism in carving.

The dominant feeling will always be the love of humanity and nature; and the love of sculpture for itself.

300 St Ives Harbour

301 *Sea form (Atlantic)* Bronze, 78 in.,
in the Museum of Fine Arts, Dallas, U.S.A.

302 *Figure*. Bronze, 71¼ in. being unveiled by the Chancellor of the University, The Duchess of Devonshire, at The Northcott Theatre, Exeter, 2 November 1967.

303 Working holiday on Tresco, Isles of Scilly, June 1967: Sir Herbert Read, Professor A. M. Hammacher, F. E. Halliday, Mrs Halliday, Priaulx Rainier, myself and my niece.

304 *Figure for landscape* Bronze, 103 in. (Coll. Joseph Hirshhorn: photographed in his garden in Connecticut, U.S.A.)

THE TATE GALLERY

305 Catalogue cover of my Retrospective Exhibition, April/May 1968 at the Tate Gallery (Illus. *Pelagos*).

306 Frontispiece and title page of the catalogue of my Retrospective Exhibition at the Tate Gallery. (Illus. *Image II*, marble)

307 Sculptures on the steps of the Tate Gallery

308 My friends and assistant team, Norman Stocker, George Wilkinson and Dicon Nance

309 Arranging the Retrospective Exhibition at the Tate Gallery, London March 1968.

310 The marble yard in my studio

University of Oxford

HE honour of the presence of

Dame Barbara Hepworth

at the ENCAENIA, on 26 June 1968 , is requested, the Hebdomadal Council having resolved to propose to the Convocation of the University that the Degree of Doctor of Letters, honoris causa, be conferred upon him on that occasion.

Registrar of the University.

311 The invitation to attend the Encaenia at Oxford on the occasion of the conferment of an Honorary Degree – Hon. D. Litt.

312 Order of Proceedings of The Encaenia at Oxford, 26 June 1968

313 The Address delivered in the Sheldonian Theatre

DAME BARBARA HEPWORTH, D.B.E.

Fuerunt sane apud antiquos poetriae et, quamvis raro, pictrices; in arte autem statuaria feminae nomen, quod sciam, non traditur: saxa enim vel ligna fortasse duriora videbantur esse quam ut femina edolaret. At dolandi artem haec capessivit, cum in Collegio Artium Regio nemo eam doceret, et scalpro aggressa vivi saxi naturam, ut ipsa ait, auscultatur, dum una cum venae pulsu malleum vibrat. Tunc abhinc annos XXXVII, dum truncum humanum sculpit, repente tutudit, pupugit, foramen aperuit, et cum foramine novum spatii intellectum expediit, ita ut in locum veteris soliditatis veniret vacuitas, ut rotatile nescioquod vacuum et palpabile evisceraretur. Aleatoria res erat, sed genio indulsit, sed magno nisu, licet aliquot sues Minervam docerent, ad normam et numerum suum perrexit.

Cum enim a figura humana esset exorsa, mox simpliciorem reddidit, ut homo in sphenidiformem avem abiret; deinde omne hominis vestigium 'abstraxit' et ad formas geometricas confugit; circulos cum quadratis maritat ut perambulare (quod tamen in glyptotheca non licet) inviteris; interdum aliquid humani, si altius repetas, subsusurrat, vel, si minus, unda, glomus, nux. Siliquam ingentem hic videres, pisis vacuam, chordis tensam, ad formam fidiculae enitentem; illic truncos condicionem Dryados (vel Dyados) capessere et saxa colloquii. Non statuas diceres sed baetulos Daedalicos, amuleta facticia, vitae superstitis symbola. At cur tempto quod latine vix fieri potest verbis ea describere quae vel Oxonii potestis intueri vel ab ipsa donata in glyptotheca Tatiana? Sufficiat dicere hanc sinceritatem et cum subtilitate simplicitatem arti reddidisse, et, dum saepius nomina Graeca indit, plus quam Graecam serenitatem.

Praesento vobis Dominam Barbaram Hepworth, dignam cuius causa inveniendae sint voces Romanis ignotae, sculptricem et plastida, Britannicae sculpturae renovatricem, assiduam cuniculariam et superficierum limatricem, ut admittatur ad gradum Doctoris in Litteris honoris causa.

Statuarum artifex insignissima, cuius doctae manus ex omni materia novas pulchritudinis formas nobis largiuntur, ego auctoritate mea et totius Universitatis admitto te ad gradum Doctoris in Litteris honoris causa.

The ancients had their poetesses and, more rarely, paintresses, but no name of a sculptress has come down to us. Marble and even wood were perhaps thought too hard for a woman to carve. But at a time when no one in the Royal College of Arts taught carving, she set herself to carve, and, in her phrase, to 'listen' to the stone as she plied her hammer in the rhythm of her heart-beats. Then thirty-seven years ago, when she was giving the final touches to a torso, she suddenly struck, pierced, and punched a hole, and with the hole released a new conception of space. In place of solidity there came emptiness, and a swirling vacuum, inviting to the touch (cf. *Forms to Touch*), was extracted. It was a gamble, but she followed her hunch, and by effort, amid some Philistine derision, won through to her own style and rhythm.

She had begun with the human figure, which she then simplified into penguin-like forms; then she 'abstracted' all trace of the representative and took to geometric shapes, marrying circles and squares, and inviting us to walk through them (cf. *Four-square walk through*, but you had better not try to in the Tate). Sometimes there is a suggestion of the human, or, if not, of a wave, a hank of wool, or a nut: here you may see a huge pod, its peas shelled, strung with cords, aspiring to the condition of a violin; there a trunk struggling to be a Dryad (or a Dyad), and menhirs to get into conversation. You can scarcely call them statues, nor does she, but prehistoric baetyls, amulets, fetishes, 'talismans for survival'. But why should I attempt what is scarcely possible in Latin, to describe what you can see, in Oxford too (in New College and St. Catherine's), or in the Tate Gallery, to which she has given nine of her works. It must be enough to say that she has given her art sincerity, and a subtle simplicity, and, amid many works with Greek names, a more than Greek serenity.

I present to you Dame Barbara Hepworth, who deserves to have invented for her those words unknown to the Romans, sculptress and modeller, 'a compulsive burrower' who produces exquisite surfaces, a renewer of British sculpture, for admission to the Degree of Doctor of Letters *honoris causa*.

Dame Barbara Hepworth is a great sculptor, whose skill has given us new forms of beauty in all kinds of material. I admit her to the Degree of Doctor of Letters.

314 In the procession of Honorary Graduands with Dr Jean Rey

I can't say much about Herbert Read. Henry Moore, Naum Gabo and Ben Nicholson have spoken so well from all our hearts. Herbert was my first sponsor and friend. For some years before his death we shared a common illness and suffering and had the same surgeons. Without him there is an awful blank. On 18 June 1968 I wrote a poem . . . in both praise and anguish.

His great courage and understanding helped me so much.

315 The painting *Marble forms* given to Lady Read and her family, inscribed *In praise of Sir Herbert Read, his poetry & eloquence, his creative silences*

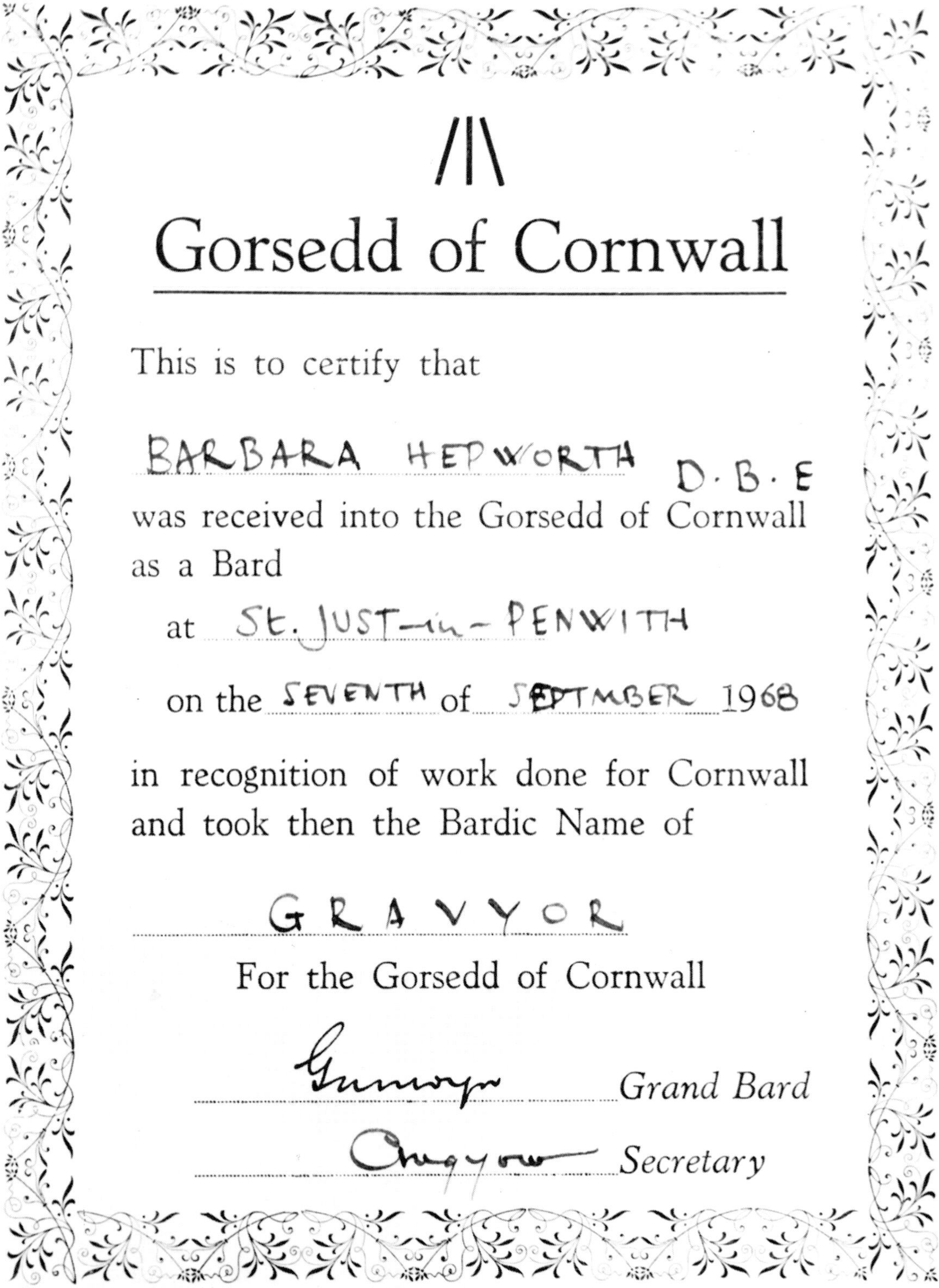

/|\

Gorsedd of Cornwall

This is to certify that

BARBARA HEPWORTH D·B·E

was received into the Gorsedd of Cornwall
as a Bard

at St. JUST-in-PENWITH

on the SEVENTH of SEPTMBER 1968

in recognition of work done for Cornwall
and took then the Bardic Name of

G R A V Y O R

For the Gorsedd of Cornwall

_____ Grand Bard

_____ Secretary

316 Certificate on being received into the Gorsedd of Cornwall as a Bard, and given the Bardic name 'Gravyor'

317 & 318 The Barding Ceremony, 7 September 1968

319 Cover of a booklet published on September 23rd when I
was granted the Honorary Freedom of the Borough of St Ives

*The invitation to attend this ceremony and
become a Bard of Cornwall moved me very
much indeed. To be so welcomed after my
years here where I have enjoyed much hospi-
tality, love and help meant more than I can say.*

*I chose the name of 'Gravyor' (sculptor)
and it was a memorable moment when this was
conferred upon me by the Grand Bard of
Cornwall at an unforgettable ceremony at St.
Just in Pentwith A fitful wind was blowing,
but the whole setting was deeply impressive. I
shall never forget the sound of singing voices,
the cadences of the Cornish language, the
sound of pipes, horn and harp.*

*I think the name 'Gravyor' suits me and
could well go on my headstone as showing my
love for this land and its people.*

BOROUGH OF ST. IVES, CORNWALL

On the occasion of the conferment of the
Honorary Freedom of the Borough on

BERNARD LEACH

BARBARA HEPWORTH

IN RECOGNITION OF
THEIR INTERNATIONAL CONTRIBUTION TO THE ARTS

BARBARA HEPWORTH

23rd SEPTEMBER, 1968

Borough of

St. Ives, Cornwall.

WE the Mayor, Aldermen and Burgesses of the Borough of St. Ives, Cornwall, in pursuance of The Local Government Act, 1933, Section 259 (2) hereby confer the Honorary Freedom of the Borough of St. Ives, Cornwall, upon

Dame
Barbara Hepworth,
D.B.E.,

in recognition of the national and international eminence she has attained in the Art of Sculpture and in acknowledgment of her distinguished service to the development of the Visual Arts during her residence in the Borough We accordingly ADMIT the said Dame Barbara Hepworth, D.B.E.,

to be an

HONORARY FREEMAN OF THE BOROUGH OF ST. IVES, CORNWALL.

GIVEN under the Corporate Seal of the Mayor Aldermen and Burgesses of the Borough this 23rd day of September, 1968.

Mayor.

Town Clerk.

320 With Bernard Leach when being received by the Mayor of St Ives, Councillor E. M. Jory

321 The Scroll given to me by the Borough of St Ives

322 The casket containing the scroll

323 Receiving the casket and scroll from the Mayor of St Ives

324 Press cutting from the *Guardian*

Cornish freedom

by NICHOLAS DE JONGH

St Ives, Cornwall.

AT 8 a.m. today workmen were making a bank of white stone and plants outside the Guildhall. St Ives was preparing to give the freedom of its borough to two distinguished citizens—Barbara Hepworth, s c u l p t o r , and Bernard Leach, potter.

It was as if the borough was at last recognising the fact that artists are pleased to come, live, and belong in this fishing port.

The giving of a freedom entails a wealth of pomp and circumstance. The programme detailing the events of the ceremony listed no fewer than 36 items of procedure from " the councillors will take their seats in the council chamber," to " the aldermen, councillors, and distinguished guests proceeding in cars for luncheon."

In the tiny council chamber, with a precarious scaffolding platform, erected for the TV cameras, 80 people crammed themselves together at 10 45 a.m. to witness the occasion. The mayor, describing Dame Barbara's art as " sparing of line," and " in touch with the Universe," pointed out in what might be called a peroration how great and international was her repute. Then Dame Barbara swore " to be true to our Sovereign Lady Queen Elizabeth." She received a casket and scroll.

In reply to the tributes she asked the assembly to " accept my most sincere thanks." " I love St Ives," Dame Barbara said. For 30 years it had been not only her physical home, it had also been her spiritual one. " I have always been part of it," she said, and in token of her appreciation she asked St Ives to accept a big sculpture.

Here no houses seem to be made of brick. They are of stone, concrete block, and granite. The rocks on the sea shore look like undisciplined equivalents of Hepworth orig-inals. It's an untamed land.

The affinity between the St Ives landscape and the Hepworth sculpture is immediately clear. It is also freely acknowledged by Hepworth herself. " St Ives," she told me, " has had a great effect on my work. It has given me tremendous strength and now suddenly it is even more terrific." For her the beauty " bursts out " all the time. The light and the sea appear different every day.

Bernard Leach, now 82 and similarly honoured, was described by the mayor as preserving a tradition of pottery acceptable to a younger generation. On his casket, in recognition of his services to Japan, were the Japanese symbols for long life and of affection.

There was lunch in honour of the two artists, more speeches at the library, and by 4 p.m. Dame Barbara had retired to bed for a short rest, exhausted, one assumes, but a free woman at last.

325 St. Ives Parish Churchyard showing part of the Open-Air Exhibition, September 1968

When Bernard Leach and I were approached to see whether we would accept the freedom of the Borough of St. Ives, I think we both felt the same – deeply touched and near to tears.

The ceremony was beautiful: quiet, with gentle words, and even the caskets and scrolls had been designed and made by local artists and craftsmen so that they were a delight to both Bernard and me.

For two weeks exhibitions of our work were staged by the Council in the town and many hundreds of people enjoyed the occasion.

I should like to thank the Town Council and The Mayor (Councillor Jory) for the exquisite taste and indeed tenderness with which they took two of St. Ives' somewhat elderly children into the fold.

326 *Dual form*. Bronze, 72⅜ in., presented to St Ives Borough Council, outside The Guildhall, St Ives

327 With Bernard Leach at St Ives Guildhall

328

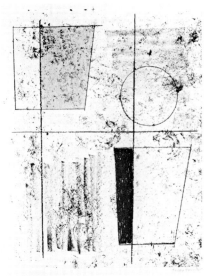

NEW LITHOGRAPHS

330

329

328 *Mycenae* (in relief), orange and black

329 *Sea forms* (relief), black and yellow

330 *Three forms assembling*, black and yellow

331 *Three oblique forms*, ochre, indigo, blue and black

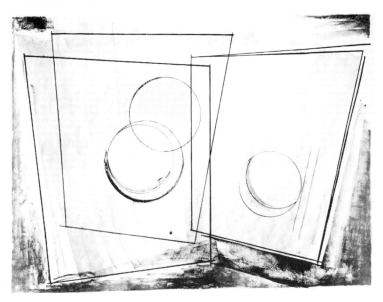

331

332 *Dual form* at The Maltings, Aldeburgh, 1968

333 *Autumn day,* mixed media

334 *Cluster of stones,* 1969

335 *Eclipse*, Acrylic and pencil

336 *Hollow form with inner form*. Bronze, 48 in.

338 *Grey shell*. Irish stone, 15¼ in.

337 *Horizontal form*. Bronze, 18⅜ in.

339 *Rhomboid*. Slate, 24 in.

Sculptors' gift to nation

A portrait of Sir Herbert Read painted by Patrick Heron in 1950 has been presented to the nation by Dame Barbara Hepworth and Henry Moore, the sculptors.

As the foremost interpreter of contemporary art, Sir Herbert was closely associated with Dame Barbara and Mr. Moore during the "exciting artistic developments of the 1930s", the National Portrait Gallery said of the gift yesterday. The portrait, now on exhibition, formerly belonged to the British Council.

340 *Two figures* (with colour). Bronze, 8ft 3in. photographed at The Morris Singer Foundry 342 Press cutting from *The Times*, 30 December 1968

341 *Three monoliths*, 1964, oil and pencil

343 *Moon form*. White marble, height 24 in.

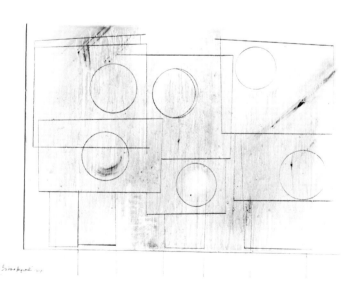

THE PROBLEM OF
INTERNATIONALISM
IN ART

This speech, the last public statement by the late Sir Herbert Read was made at The Cultural Congress of Havana, in January 1968.

In the past fifty years two developments have taken place that have as their aim the promotion of an international style in the arts. In the capitalist world the motive is economic: art has become an international commodity and works of art now rival gold as a medium of exchange. Art dealers, like bankers, now have their branches or agents in every great city in the Western World. To meet the demands of an international market art is now subject to international methods of promotion and distribution. Various mass-media of communication — the press, art books, illustrated magazines and television — give hot news to artists, their dealers and the public of any change in fashion or reputation.

The motive behind a similar phenomenon in the communist countries is political. Art is conceived as a powerful instrument of propaganda; the State requires artists to serve the supreme revolutionary purpose, spreading a clearly defined programme of education and idealism by means of a style known as 'socialist realism'. Art is no longer the expression of a personal vision or of a subjective experience; it becomes an objective record of contemporary events. Such an art is also international in its scope and uniform in its style.

The final years

Barbara Hepworth died in a fire in her studio in St Ives on 20 May 1975. She was 72, and had been in poor health for some years, though this had not prevented her from working as intensively as ever. She was particularly interested in multi-part sculptures, returning in her last years to a theme that she had often explored before. Her ideas found expression in two groups of marble carvings – the Assembly of Sea Forms *(no. 347) and her last major work,* Fallen Images *(no. 354) – and in two monumental bronze compositions –* The Family of Man, *or* Nine Figures on a Hill *(no. 349) and the* Conversation with Magic Stones, *which has a deliberately retrospective quality, embodying forms first made in the nineteen-thirties and nineteen-fifties.*

After her death, Dame Barbara's studio and garden in St Ives were opened as a small museum in her memory, and in 1980 the artist's executors, following the wishes of the artist and of her daughters, gave the museum and its contents to the nation, placing it in the care of the Trustees of the Tate

345 Naum Gabo, Henry Moore and Barbara Hepworth at a preview in the Tate Gallery on 10 March 1970 of works presented to the gallery in memory of Sir Herbert Read by these artists and Ben Nicholson

Gallery. Two of the important last works, the Conversation, *and* Fallen Images, *are now on permanent public display, together with a representative group of sculptures from every period of her long career, and in all the different materials in which she worked. Her workshops remain exactly as they were, with unfinished sculptures on the stands.*

In the Winter 1974–75 Dame Barbara had been discussing the preparation of a new edition of the Pictorial Autobiography with Anthony Adams and myself. Some of the items were already chosen: others have now been added to complete the account.

ALAN BOWNESS

347 *Assembly of sea forms* White marble, height 33¼ in.

346 (left) *Theme and Variations* (1970). Bronze, height 11¼ ft, width 25 ft. Unveiled at Cheltenham in September 1972

348 The artist with Sir John Wolfenden and the Lord Mayor and Lady Mayoress at the opening of the Barbara Hepworth exhibition at Plymouth, 16 June 1970

349 *The Family of Man* (*nine figures on a hill*) (1970). Bronze

350 With her seven grandchildren at her 70th birthday party in St Ives, January 1973

352 In Trewyn Studio garden, Spring 1973

SCULPTRESS Dame Barbara Hepworth rounded off her 70th birthday last night with a party at the Tregenna Castle, a hotel near her studio home in St. Ives. Cornwall, where greetings from all over the world had been arriving throughout the day.

She has worked in St. Ives for more than 30 years,

351 Press cutting from the *Evening Standard*, 11 January 1973

353 Presentation of Honorary Membership of the American Academy of Arts & Letters and the National Institute of Arts & Letters to Dame Barbara Hepworth and Sir Michael Tippett at the U.S. Embassy, London, 4 June 1973

354 *Fallen images* White marble, height 36 in. The artist's last major work (1974)

355 *Lotus* White marble, height 30½ in. (1973–4)

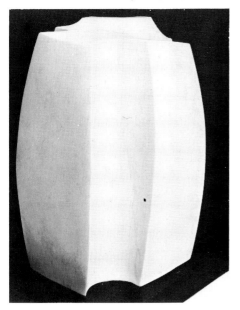

Dame Barbara dies in fire

DAME Barbara Hepworth, aged 73, the sculptress, died last night in a fire at her studio home, Trewyn, near the centre of St Ives, Cornwall, where she had lived and worked for about 25 years. Her body was found by firemen in the ground floor room leading into the garden. It was in this room that she did most of her work. Recently she had been badly handicapped by arthritis.

The death of Dame Barbara Hepworth removes one of Britain's foremost sculptors. Her works remain as a reminder of her unequalled greatness as a master of abstract sculpture. Her genius built for her a great international reputation and in the galleries of London, Zurich, Paris, Oslo, Copenhagen, Munich, and even farther afield her sculpture was acclaimed.

356 Press cutting from the *Guardian*, 21 May 1975

357 Interior of The Barbara Hepworth Museum, 1976
358 Garden of The Barbara Hepworth Museum

FOR BARBARA HEPWORTH

In stone and bone and bronze and blood
in the wild heartbeat and the sobbing sea
lie the thought and the passion.

With hammer and eye and chisel and hand
with the cool of mind and the warmth of heart
the Sculptor's love makes manifest.

ANTHONY ADAMS

359 Obituary notice from the *Guardian*, 21 May 1975

Great abstract art

Emancipation has enabled many women to participate creatively in the cultural life of this century. Even among these many, Dame Barbara Hepworth's career has been an outstanding one. She was probably the most significant woman artist in the history of art to this day, and it is all the more remarkable that this eminence should have been achieved by an Englishwoman and in the field of sculpture. To contribute significantly to the wide world of art from a British studio in the 1930s and 1940s, and more particularly to take a leading rôle in the revitalising of what had here become almost moribund art, took driving energy and the right kind of ambition, as well as a rare and particular talent.

To this her Yorkshire origins may well have contributed. Barbara Hepworth was born in Wakefield in 1903 and attended the Wakefield Girls' High School. A scholarship took her to Leeds School of Art, another to the Royal College of Art in London, and a third enabled her to travel in Italy. When she first showed her work, in 1928, it consisted mostly of massive, simplified torsos, but by the early thirties her paraphrase of the human body had taken on landscape qualities: both sorts of natural form continued into her completely abstract work of the middle

OBITUARY

thirties and after giving warmth and intimacy to forms that tended towards geometry.

She settled in St Ives in 1939, and remained there for the rest of her life. She ventured out to travel across the world as her mounting international fame required of her, but was happiest in the semi-seclusion of her home and studio overlooking town and harbour. She became a great defender of the beauties of Cornwall, as also she worked for the advancement of art in Britain through her work as Tate Gallery trustee and in other rôles. Her sculpture was soon enriched and refined by forms suggestive of the action of the sea and by the Cornish light. In her later years it sometimes tended towards the monumental, partly in response to commissions for sculpture in an architectural setting. It may be doubted whether these occasions suited her special gifts best. At any rate she returned often to making smaller pieces, between hand size and human size, and it is in these that her artistic character seems most persuasively expressed.

Its most remarkable quality was its pervading, unselfconscious femininity. However stringent the forms she used, her work is always marked by an ultimate kindness and gentleness, and often by a particular gesture of sheltering, embracing. When she uses two or more elements grouped together there is an unmistakable sense of human intercourse.

She was married twice, to the sculptor John Skeaping and to Ben Nicholson by whom she had triplets.